Blow My Blues Away

LOUISIANA STATE UNIVERSITY PRESS
Baton Rouge

Blow My Blues Away

George Mitchell

To my mother

ISBN 0-8071-0416-7

Library of Congress Catalog Card Number: 72-119111

Copyright © 1971 by Louisiana State University Press

All rights reserved

Manufactured in the United States of America

Designed by Albert R. Crochet

Foreword

The poor tempt us in ways we often enough simply are not aware of. We hear of them or cast a look here and there at them and we allow ourselves the satisfaction of immediate outrage, horror, sadness, and pity; or we scorn them for not somehow, anyhow, getting out of such circumstances. Alternatively, we may take yet another tack and ironically grant them more than all other people: special courage, an unusual measure of wisdom and grace, an exceptional deepness of mind and warmth of heart. All those apparently contradictory responses seem prompted by a common assumption: they are different, these people, not only because they lack money but because that lack, sustained over the generations, causes all sorts of distinctive changes in people—changes in the way they think about the world and about themselves, changes in how they get along with one another and in sum live, or at least try to live. Those changes eventually consolidate themselves into—well, the words and phrases are all about us these days: a culture, a culture of poverty, a kind of social structure, a state of disadvantage and deprivation, which of course have "psychological correlates," or so I've heard it put. If the social scientists seem cold and brittle and even a bit unfriendly, there are always the so-called (and self-styled) humanists, who glory in "the nobility of these people." That's what I heard said again and again in Mississippi's Delta during 1964 and 1965, when hundreds of northerners came South to live with sharecroppers and tenant farmers and the small-town poor of the state. Nervously, arrogantly, smugly, generously (and they would have the gall to talk about their generosity) the judgments were made, and here is one of them from one of my tapes:

> Look, you have to challenge your own stereotypes. You can't be stingy—you know, intellectually stingy. You have to be generous; you have to see their good side, how beautiful they can be. They are great people, greater than any other people I've ever met. They are aristocrats, you know; that's what they are. They have a real philosophical view of life, and they refuse to get involved in the petty details that other people spend their time with. That's what an aristocrat is, a man who can transcend the usual limits.

Well-meaning, self-sacrificing, hard-working, he was awed by the people he so lavishly praised and he wanted nothing but the best for them, an aristocrat's position if that could at all be managed. Yet, he failed then, and on other occasions as well, to see how tired and bored and boring and angry and petulant and silly and rude those same people could be—even as the rest of us are from time to time. He also failed to realize that such people do not "refuse to get involved in petty details." They have no such choice. They have to contend with a life that constantly forces them to take nothing for granted, to accept the unacceptable, submit to the unavoidable, make do with the awful, and rejoice in what is left: sheer life itself, still somewhat around, still better than death, still capable of offering a good moment here and there, now and then. Nobility may indeed be measured by the suffering that people manage to confront and through it all stay alive; but the price paid is high, and the injuries strike at everything—at the body, but also the mind and heart and soul.

I say this here because George Mitchell has done well to bring up immediately in *Blow My Blues Away* the whole vexing matter of what poverty "does" (if that is the word) to its victims (and that is certainly only *one* of the suitable words). He knows that the people he met and heard and came to love so very much, and so openly and unashamedly, are a mixed lot; that each of them is full of contradictions and ambiguities; and that if we *all* are a mixed lot and full of inconsistencies, at least some of us can cover things up better, conceal a lot—in fact, so very much—from others and, alas, from ourselves. So, Mitchell makes clear that the South possesses—yes, even after the loss of so many of its best workers to the North's ghettos—thousands upon thousands of terribly poor, hungry, sad, hurt, bewildered, ailing, idle, frightened people, many of whom, at the same time, show themselves to be intelligent, discerning, imaginative, resourceful, and full of just what Christ urged upon us all: guile.

Guile informs the blues, the field songs and work songs, the spirituals that the people we meet in this fine book sing and sing and sing. Just how much guile I doubt anyone knows—because after so many decades, after hundreds of years in fact, both whites and blacks have come to rely upon guile as a virtual means of encounter and mutual survival: the guile of the powerful owner who feigns innocence and worse; the guile of the bossed and weak and needy, who feign another kind of innocence, the kind that takes the form of a willingness, even an eagerness to do what has to be done, say what can only be said, and act in whatever way one must. Then come the moments of truth—when the powerful get nervous and brandish their guns, and when the poor get nervous (and weary and resigned and terribly gloomy) and, among other things, break out into song, into music, into rhythms and cries and shouts and exclamations and appeals and sighs and moans and tears and piercing, wrenching sounds.

We owe a lot to George Mitchell. He and his wife offer us in *Blow My Blues Away* a beautiful book, full of all the doubt and beauty and despair and richness and misery of southern black people. For me the book was an unforgettable experience: since 1958 I have either lived in Mississippi (for two years) or gone back there (at least three times a year) and until I saw the manuscript of this book I found the state and its people hard to comprehend, for all that has been written about them. Now, at least some of those people can be known by all of us —seen and read about and, I gather, heard. I only wish more of my colleagues

—more social scientists, more anthropologists, or psychiatrists, or whatever —might find it in themselves to work as Mitchell did; and more important, think as he does; and even more important, write as he does—openly, honestly, without pretense, without fake and dense mumbo jumbo.

The author has more than a touch of the poet in him. He knows how to bring alive the people he obviously feels so drawn to. Nor is he ashamed to make his affections clear, to mix his own values and sentiments with those of these people—who became his friends, it would appear. When I think of all the cold, precious, self-important "studies" (of this "group" and that one) I come across in all those professional journals, not to mention books, I have to wonder why it is that we have become what we have become—so afraid of, so shy of the very people we travel from so far in order to be with and observe and get to know. Mitchell, though, went to Mississippi as a witness, and I am using the word in its religious and philosophical senses. I say witness and not student or professional man or scientist or "participant-observer" or even social reformer. He went—I gather—because of his own ideals, but also because he was drawn, enchanted, moved to go. He went because he wanted to see and hear, and make others look and listen. He went because he believed that part of man's destiny could be caught sight of, overheard—if only we would, each of us, pay respectful attention and reach out and allow ourselves to be instructed. Having gone and learned, he has chosen to share with us his discovery: that men and women who a good deal of the time have little cause for hope still manage to assert their passions with great fervor and insistence and boldness and directness, and in do-

ing so assert also their humanity. I know that this vivid, almost haunting book is full of what we in the academy call social history and psychological "observations" and sociological "data" from the "field." Yet there is something else here that I hope none of us forgets to acknowledge: a sensitive artist's effort to give coherence to something he has found uncommonly touching, moving, important. In this instance that "something" is a number of somebodies, who despite everything wrong and bad and evil and treacherous they have met up with, despite their all too apparent invisibility and their frequently mentioned namelessness, are just that: somebodies, and somebodies we will now feel closer to because of *Blow My Blues Away.*

ROBERT COLES, M.D.

Harvard University
University Health Services

ix

Preface

My wife and I took our first trip to Mississippi during the summer of 1967 to record, interview, and photograph those black musicians of the Delta area, whose special mode of expression—country blues—is fast disappearing.

In regard to method and format, the reason for the musical setting of the book—other than the preservation of an intriguing form of music—is a practical one. My interest in their music opened doors to homes whose residents otherwise might have been suspicious and helped break down at least some of the barriers of communication which usually exist between black man and white man. (Nevertheless, it must constantly be kept in mind that the comments of the people speaking on these pages were made in response to a middle-class white's questions.)

Each person was interviewed after he or she had sung and played for some time into my microphone. Jessie Mae Brooks, Ada Mae Anderson, and William Diamond were interviewed three times, in 1967, 1968, and 1969; Rosa Lee Hill and Robert Diggs were interviewed twice, in 1967 and 1968, as was Other Turner, in 1967 and 1969; Robert Johnson was interviewed once, in 1969. Only their responses to my questions are included here, although when I felt the nature of the question was important, I let them repeat it in the text.

My wife and I attended two services at New Salem Baptist Church and two barbecues at L. P. Buford's store, and the photographs and events are combined into one account in each case and are described as accurately as the absence of a tape recorder would permit. (The songs presented in the chapter on the church service might not have been sung when we were there, although members of the church sang them for us later so they could be included.)

Every photograph is where it belongs: pictures of houses are of the musicians' houses; pictures of other people are of their families or friends, or residents of their area; pictures of the land are of the countryside surrounding their houses.

The last chapter is composed of transcriptions of verses from songs performed by musicians we recorded on our trips, including some by those interviewed for the book and some by those who weren't. Some of the verses are original compositions; some have been commercially recorded before; others are traditional. Because the written word cannot serve as a substitute for actually hearing the music, the reader might be interested in the two volumes of records from my tapes, "Mississippi Delta Blues," issued on Arhoolie Records. Music from my tapes is also on "Robert Nighthawk and Houston Stackhouse," on Testament, and on a future release on Origin Jazz Library of bluesmen in the Bentonia, Mississippi, area. Rosa Lee Hill can be heard on Atlantic's "The Blues Roll On," produced by Alan Lomax, who also recorded Sidney Hemphill.

I owe thanks to many people. David Evans of the anthropology department at California State College at Fullerton supplied me with many leads in Mississippi, without which our trips would not have been the successes they were.

The book probably would have never been written were it not for my wife Cathy. In Mississippi, her enthusiasm equaled my own, and she never tired of our constant search for new musicians. At home, through her transcriptions, proofreading, advice, and optimistic encouragement, she made the production of the book possible.

Most of all I owe thanks to those who really wrote this book—the people of Mississippi who spent many hours talking and singing into my microphone, leading us to other sources, and generally making us feel at home. In particular, I want to thank Rosa Lee Hill, who did not live (she died in late 1968) to see her indomitable outlook on life in print, Jessie Mae Brooks, Ada Mae Anderson, Other Turner, Fred McDowell, William Diamond, Abe McNeil, L. P. Buford, and the Reverend M. B. Chaney.

For the book's faults, I can, of course, thank only myself.

Contents

Blow My Blues Away

Introduction

"Afro-American music," wrote Paul Oliver, "may well be considered the one indigenous gift of the modern Americas to the world's art." Ironically, however, it did not grow directly out of the abundant society for which America is known. It grew out of the peculiar experience of one of this country's most oppressed groups of people—black Americans—and it traditionally satisfied needs which could be satisfied in few other ways.

Work songs and field hollers helped alleviate the tedium of the field hand or railroad worker. Spirituals gave the oppressed Negro courage to continue living under seemingly unbearable hardships and strengthened his belief that he would find relief in the hereafter. African fife and drum music lent country picnics and barbecues a certain gaiety and provided rhythms and moods for those who wanted to dance some of the frustrations out of their systems. And country blues, that intensely personal music, helped satisfy strong emotional needs through the individual expression of the singer's own experiences—his loves, hates, good fortune, disappointments.

Jazz, soul, rock-and-roll, and psychedelic music—offshoots of work songs, spirituals, and country blues—are accepted and often performed in the white world, and are frequently heard in con-

3

cert halls and nightclubs and over the radio and television. But the contributions of Afro-American music as it was first sung and played have been recognized only by a relatively small number of whites such as Paul Oliver, and it has been heard mostly on the front porches of shacks of Mississippi sharecroppers, or in ramshackle rural churches, or at Saturday evening barbecues in the country.

The reader has probably noticed by now that I have used the past tense in describing rural Negro music. The music is rapidly becoming extinct as the particular conditions which produced it are disappearing. One of the regions where it is most widely played and sung at present is northwest Mississippi—in the delta of the Yazoo and Mississippi rivers. Like the Delta's stark landscape, the condition of most rural blacks in this area has changed little during the past century. But, even here, the effects of northern migration, of mass communi-

cations, and of the decline of the cotton economy have been felt. As one side effect, the music is dying and dying rapidly. Older musicians have laid down their instruments, and the young people laugh at "that old stuff." Most of the singers and musicians still active are in their forties and fifties; when they die, so also will their music.

This book has two related purposes: to document a dying music and to introduce the reader to the rural black person as an individual, with his own fears, his own joys, his own hangups, his own hopes, instead of a member of a group whose collective "characteristics" are so often studied, analyzed and put into numbers. (Of course, the frequently noted sociological, historical, and psychological forces concerning "the Negro" are obvious here, but they come alive in individual terms in the words of people who themselves are affected by them.)

What relevance, the reader may ask

when he gets into the interview chapters of this book, does a person's childhood memories, his job, religious beliefs, his experiences with the opposite sex, and his hopes for the future have for his music? The answer to this question is that the music of the people the reader is about to meet is intricately tied in with their lives, feelings, and experiences. Their thoughts are the themes of their songs. The emotions they express are the soul of their music.

Most books and articles on bluesmen have attempted to trace the influencing factors on particular musicians' styles and so have been of the "where-did-he-live, who-did-he-know" type. But, in my opinion, they have shortchanged the network of blues enthusiasts across the world insofar as they have failed to bring out the true sources of a bluesman's music.

This is not to say these writings have nothing to offer; they have a great deal to offer and are invaluable for any blues lover. It is only to say that *Blow My Blues Away* is not intended merely to add to the research of folklorists and blues researchers. For these, the reader is referred to books by Paul Oliver and Samuel B. Charters and to such periodicals as *Blues Unlimited* and *Blues World*. Oliver's books also offer insight into the experiences that have produced this music, but they primarily focus on musicians who were recorded by commercial companies. In this respect, too, *Blow My Blues Away* differs from most other writings on the subject (*Been Here and Gone* by Frederic Ramsey and *The Rainbow Sign* by Alan Lomax being the major exceptions).

Blues, after all, was truly part of the fabric of everyday living for thousands of rural blacks. More than simply a form of music, blues is the music of a people.

5

1/ *Been Here All My Days*

The Mississippi Delta and the surrounding country in this northwestern section of the state are home to the blues and the people who live them.

The lowlands alongside the Mississippi River, the Delta proper, are flat and monotonous. Between the highway and the horizons of the endless cotton fields can be seen only an occasional shack squatting among the plants or a woman hunched over the land with a hoe in her hands. Daredevil pilots in Piper Cubs barely miss the dilapidated buildings as they swoop down over the fields, spraying the plants against the dreaded boll weevil. Everywhere, the stink of pesticides permeates the summer air. There are few trees to help soak up the stifling heat. The nights are not much cooler, bringing only a little relief to the black people, whose homes are unprotected from the relentless sun during the day.

Farther to the east, on the fringe of the Delta, the cotton fields begin to disappear as the land bulges into knotty hills. Kudzu vine conquers everything it comes near, transforming the trees that line the winding highway into green stalagmites. Rusty barbed-wire fences surround most of the houses, and gates are closed.

Unnamed dirt or gravel roads ramble throughout the Mississippi countryside. For the rural Negro living along them life has changed little during the last fifty years. He still keeps the water he draws from the nearest well in a wooden barrel on his front porch. His wife still cooks on a wood stove. He still has to walk out back to the outhouse if there is one (if not, he "slips around the side of the house").

He may even have less to eat than he

did in earlier years. The refrigerator is usually empty, except perhaps for a can of potted meat. He often eats no more than one meal a day, which may consist of collard greens and a chunk of cornbread. Although his house is run-down and almost devoid of modern conveniences, the chances are good that pride in himself shows in many small ways. Discarded tires form a fence around flowers growing in the front yard. If the ground is too hard-packed and impoverished, flowers bloom in rusty lard buckets. Little bouquets of dried onions hang from the sagging rafters of the porch.

The interior of the rural Negro's tiny two-room house is often tidy and spotless. The warped, gray floors are well scrubbed; the sheets on his beds are without wrinkles; clothes are hung neatly on nails or packed away in trunks. Colorful magazine pages or unmatched strips of faded wallpaper cover the walls.

Artificial flowers, assorted trinkets, old photographs, dated calendars, and religious pictures decorate the rooms. He and his family have done their best to conceal the deprivations and wants in their lives.

Of course, the house down the road might not be as well kept. After years of nothing but squalor, the down-and-out family has become so demoralized that they are oblivious to the filth in which their lives are smothered. The dungeon-like dwelling, dark and musty, reeks of the peculiar stench of poverty. Nine or ten children, whose grimy clothes blend into the dirt on their bodies, are buried at night in mattress stuffing rotting from the workings of rats. Empty wine bottles, once filled with corn whiskey, litter the floor. Flies swarm over pots and pans, dishes and scraps in the kitchen. The woman of the house long ago has

given up trying to keep livable the shack, which she can only hope to leave.

The most significant change in the lives of most of these people during the last decade has been the growing scarcity of jobs and the resultant worsening of living conditions. Thirty years ago almost every black man was a farmer of one type or another—a sharecropper, a farm laborer or, if he was lucky, a farmer for himself. Although a few sporadically still pick and "chop" cotton today—usually for forty or fifty cents an hour—huge machines are rapidly replacing the hand laborer. The poor man, who for years has depended on the land for his livelihood, is becoming virtually useless and almost forgotten in the process.

The more fortunate ones work in town as filling station attendants, dishwashers, or janitors. Better jobs are even harder to come by. As one farm laborer reflected:

There is so many people in Mississippi that just ain't qualified for the jobs that open up. You take that aluminum plant up there. I'll tell you about that application—you gotta take a test and work fractions and all that. Now where maybe I can do it, there are nine more that can't. I may can do it, and then there's another fellow with a bigger family than I got. Well, he got to take care of his family. But he ain't got no job; can't use him.

It's done got so now that you just naturally has to have a lot of education to get a job near about. If you ain't got a good education, you just can't hardly get nary'n. Now what people going do that ain't qualified to get them jobs and got a family to take care of? What are they going do? If they leave Mississippi, they're still going have the same problem up North.

But scores of young people are leaving Mississippi for what they hope will be a better life in northern cities. The num-

12

ber of men and women between the ages of twenty and thirty-five seen in the towns and the countryside is strikingly small. "My son says after he gets out of the Army, he going leave Mississippi and ain't never coming back," a father rooted in Mississippi says with a touch of pride and envy. "I'd leave myself, I would, if I thought I'd do any better up there for my family. Been here all my days." And the many abandoned shacks testify to the fact that large numbers are leaving.

The small towns which dot the Delta and the hill country seem almost deserted on weekdays. But "going to town" on weekends is the major recreation for the men. A few play checkers on the courthouse lawn. Some sit on benches outside the barbershop. Others get drunk in the ramshackle cafes that line the streets of the "colored section."

Still others congregate at homes of friends who have tolerant wives. It is not uncommon for twenty or thirty men to crowd into a two-room shack. The booze flows freely and the dice roll incessantly.

Although today radios play in shacks and jukeboxes bellow in cafes, many black people in Mississippi still make their own music or search out friends who do. However, the number of people who make music is diminishing and many who formerly played have stopped.

14

But the old songs have not yet died in Mississippi.

It is often said that blues was born in Mississippi, and this may be true. Where a harsh life afforded no other means for providing entertainment, gaining prestige, or shedding frustrations, the blues filled a vacuum.

The blues singer often composes or "studies" his own songs, singing about whatever is on his mind at the time. His songs may be morose, merry, bitter, or bawdy. Usually accompanying himself on guitar or harmonica, he sings of hard times and easy money, good loving and cheating women, restless rambling and grinding toil.

Although blues is the most popular type of music, jumps, ballads, and work songs have also been passed on from generations before. Drum and fife bands make a haunting, primitive sound at barbecues and picnics. And, whether ac-

companied by musical instruments or not, whether in church or at home, spiri-

tuals or "church songs" still bring solace
to a troubled people.

2/ Other Turner

Como, population 789, is a quiet town. Interstate 55 streams past on one side, while Highway 51 rambles along on the other. Half the storefronts along the lifeless business district are boarded up. The only public bathroom is in the one-room city hall across the street. A hand-scrawled sign in the window of Mrs. M. V. Perkins' store reads: "Pay your burial dues here."

Go down the blacktop past the comfortable white residences, take a left onto the gravel road at the third hill, go over the narrow, wooden bridge at "Honey-Do Corner," turn right at the old schoolhouse, and you are at Other Turner's house. About eight bony mongrels loll at the foot of the front steps. Plows, saddles, mule hitches, old wagons are scattered in the yard.

Other (pronounced Oh-thur) is a member of Como's fife and drum band—playing fife, brass drum, and snare drum alternately. People around Panola and Tate counties prefer drum bands over any other type of music at weekend picnics and barbecues. Drums are better to dance to.

Other is a serious, earnest man; he rarely smiles. When he plays music, he doesn't like any fooling around. He is a proud man—proud of his musician-

ship, proud of working hard to support his family, proud of always being "straight."

I was raised without a father. I was about three months old when my mother and father separated. When she left my father, she was carrying me in her arms and we left from down there in Rankin County, Mississippi, and went to Free Springs to an old place they call Egypt

and I was raised there. I'm fifty now so that was about fifty years ago.

The first time I seed my father after that, I was seventeen years old, walking down the big road. He didn't even know me. I was walking right beside my mother and my older sister. He was just down on a visit, I guess, or something. And he saw us in the road, riding a red bay horse. He said, "Good morning," and I said, "Good morning."

He said, "Betty . . ." She says, "Yeah?" He says, "This is you?" She said, "This is me, Hollis."

He says, "Where has you been?" She says, "Oh, 'round about, trying to make it. But I got the good Master with me and I'm going to make it."

(That's my motto now. If you try, you can make it. Put your hand in God's hand and believe and don't give up. Keep trying. The way is open.)

He got down and shook hands with

her. My sister Rose was standing there and he said, "What girl is this you got with you?" She said, "Ah, Hollis, this is your daughter."

He said, "Ah, you're joking. That ain't none of my daughter." He said, "Rosie?" She said, "Sir?" Said, "Do you know me?" She said, "No, sir."

He shook his head, said, "Oh, oh." He went to crying. He said, "Lord, have mercy. Do you mean to tell me that these here are my kids? And you been gone from me that long and you done raised them by yourself?"

"Come here, baby." He patted her on the shoulder and went to crying. Said, "What young man is that over there?" She said, "That's no man, that's a boy."

"Well, who is he?" She said, "This is Other. This is your baby, Hollis." He turned his head and he said, "This ain't none of my baby." She say, "It is."

He said, "Come on up here." And I walked up. He said, "Do you know me?" I said, "No, sir."

He said, "Why?" I said, "I just don't know you."

"Betty says that you are my baby. That's all I ever know." Said, "And you're my daddy? This you, Pa?" He said, "Yeah." I said, "How you getting along?" Said, "I'm doing all right, son."

And then he looked at me. Said, "You've made a nice young man." I said, "Well, I thanks you for it." He said, "Are you going to stay with me awhile?" I said, "I guess so." He said, "I want you to stay with me forever."

I said, "Nope, I can't leave Mama." Said, "Why?" I said, "That's my daddy and my mother too. She raised me up to where I'm at now. I can't throw her away, ain't going throw her away."

He said, "Well, I'll do what I can for you."

I said, "I don't doubt it. I believe you

would. But still, that's my mother, and she's going to be my mother until she leaves here." And I stayed with her until she did left and I buried her.

Well, I was 'round thirty, and she was sick, she was ailing, and I went and got her and brought her to my house. She was sitting down on the porch. And she got weak then. She called me, said, "Other, come here, son." I walked on over. I said, "Mama, what is it? How're you feeling?" She said, "I'm feeling all right." She said, "Look, I've got something I want to tell you." I said, "What is that?"

She said, "Mama going leave you. I can't stay with you always. I've prayed to the good Lord to let me live to see you get grown to be a man. And I give you the best instruction, the best intention to raise you, and for you to get up a man to be out on your own."

She said, "Son?" I said, "Ma'am?"

22

"Be particular." I said, "Yes, ma'am. I will."

She said, "Well, Rosie and Bernice"—them are my two sisters—"I want you to be a father for them just like you was my husband. I birthed you to the world, you is my kid. You act just like a father to them. You is a father, a man amongst men, among boys growing up, you never give me a minute's trouble in your life. So if I'm gone, I want you take the other kids and do what you can until they gets out on their own. Put me away nice when I leaves here, 'cause my hand's in God's and I got my business fixed. Don't you worry about it. But take care of the rest of them."

See, my sisters weren't too young, but they was separated from their husbands, and I did just like I was their father. I was the father of them until they made a way to look out for theirselves, you see. That's what I did for them, just be a lookout for them. And just like my family here now, what I say goes.

That's the way it happened. And I never told them nothing wrong. I don't believe in that. It's two sides in anything, and that's right and wrong. If you do right, you go successful, but you cannot get any success from wrong. You cannot.

Well, my mother died about a month after she told me that. I was sorry, real sorry. That was all I had was gone, I thought at that time, but the Man that was giving me the breath to think all that, He's still with me. That's the good Lord. You can't beat it.

I'll tell you, my mother was a nice woman, smooth, settled woman, just a church woman. She was at home. Always found Betty at home, always chastizing us at home. And trying to work and vouch and make a living for us. She looked out for us all the time.

She was just nice and kind and moth-

23

ering and just treated me nice. And give me various instruction and she never did lead me nothing wrong, and if she caught me doing something wrong, she'd teach me what was right. And make me get up and wash my face and put my clothes on and visit the church—go to Sunday school. That was my mother. She didn't like no bawling, no kind of nothing like that. You had to be right. And she had a reputation from Free Springs smack on into Brandon, Mississippi, and all into Goshen Springs. Betty Turnich was one good woman. That's right, white and colored gives her that. And she could get help from anybody, any man she walked up to his face and asked for a favor, she got it. And Other's about the same way, just about.

Now she was raised up by my grandfather—Hardy Turnich. He was a dark, heavy-set man, heavy moustache. He always give me good advice and I was raised up under that and I've been that way ever since. He gave good advice: Take care of yourself, be particular, tend to your business, just let the other fellow's alone. It takes you twelve months to tend to yours. Son, be good. Be careful, be mindful of how you treat people. Treat people like you wish to be treated. And you're successful. And on until now, since I come to be a man, I don't bother nobody, I don't mistreat nobody. What I do, I tries to do good, no evil in my heart. What I do, I've tried to help people, tried to do good, speak a good word for them. No enemies, I don't want that.

My grandfather, he raised one son and three daughters, Betty, Nettie, and Maggie. And he never did have to whip them, just talk to 'em, kindly talk to 'em. That was a whipping for them.

Now my mother, though, she'd give me some whippings. The first whipping I got for chopping cotton. When she went to cook dinner, I stopped and went to playing. Out in the field, playing. Set my foot down, raked dirt up on it, make frog beds, and pulled my foot out. Said, "Look at it! Look at the hole there! See, that's a frog bed." I got a whipping about that.

The next thing I got a whipping about—chopping cotton and I stopped. Some crows was coming over—"Aaeeee, aeeeeee." I called my sister over, and I said, "Hey?" And she said, "Huh?" I said, "Lookee here, what's that going yonder?" She said, "That's a crow." I can't say what I told her. I'm not supposed to say that, now.

Well, okay, I'll tell you. At the end, I said, "What's that?" She said, "That's a crow." I said, "Kiss his ass and let him go." (Now, I wasn't suppose to say that, I didn't want to say that.) So, we had a big laugh over it. Mama's chopping cotton and she said, "What's the matter back there?" But my sister, she said, "Mama, he told me, 'There go a crow, kiss his ass and let him go.'" She said, "Don't you ever let me hear you say that no more." She tore me up about that. I begged off her, but she wouldn't let me off.

See, when I came along, my mother—she was a farmer, farmed herself—she raised me, she didn't have no husband, and I was raised up without a father. I was the man; catched the mules, go to the field, chop cotton, plow, feed the hogs, get the cows up, cut, store and haul wood, done everything I could to keep the strain off my mother. That's what I did.

But kids now—school bus running, get the clothes on, catch the bus and ride. I had to walk mine. Come back home, the same thing next morning. To the same old schoolhouse—birds flying through the cracks, lizards crawling up and down the logs, I'm jumping, couldn't study on

my lessons, looking at them lizards and things and jumping.

"What you looking at?" There go a lizard. "You'd better get your lessons!"

"Yes, ma'am!"

See, I missed schooling there. But the kids now, the school bus running and blow, they gets on and goes to school and come back, eats their dinner, study their lessons, and play around, and next day the same thing.

But I didn't have the privilege to do that. I come up the hard way. Out in the thickets and things, you couldn't hardly see across them plows and bushes, birds whistling, sun shining, hot, and I'm out there and Mama's got a switch sticking up in her apron, leading the row, chopping, me behind. Quit in the evening, come home, get our work up, sometimes be six and seven o'clock at night before we'd eat our supper.

Well, I'll just tell you what I enjoyed as a kid—I enjoyed working. What I mean by that, if I didn't work, I didn't get nothing. But if I worked, I could show something on the table in the morning. Ain't like it is now. We worked the hard way. Man! I went out and pulled fodder all day long. Pulled it all day long and tied it up in little bands. My mother be standing in the shade tree there. She tied it up in big bundles, and we go to the store and get a little four-pound bucket of lard, piece of cheese, piece of boloney sausage, some sausage in a paper sack, just grease leaking out on the ground

sometimes. Go on home. I was happy. Had me something to eat in the morning. "Mom, Mom, I'm hungry. I'm tired of playing. I want something to eat." When I'm full, I don't care nothing about playing. If I'm hungry, I can't play.

But we had a plenty to eat. Plenty! Yessir. My mother raised us like that. She'd raise hogs, kill 'em, plenty of chickens, kill a beef, and sorghum molasses, and plenty of it in the barrel. We lived just as happy, happier than we do now. With no cost on it. Didn't have to buy anything like that then. We raised it —buy just a little sugar and coffee, stuff like that. We raised our living at home.

Well, it looks tough now because people ain't got good jobs and they don't try to raise nothing at home now. They ain't interested in a garden, watermelon patches, pea patches, and potato patches. They ain't interested in none of it. Ain't got a head of cabbage in the garden.

27

They ain't interested in the home like they was when my mother raised me.

Now, the fellow, every time he turn around, he's jamming his hand in his pockets. He won't even fish. Now he's baiting his hook with a dollar. I rather take my hook and go out and fish all day and catch me a mess of fish and come on home. But now he bait his hook with a dollar. Buys fish.

The younger generation, the biggest majority of 'em, they's on fast time. That's all he wants. He ain't trying to learn nothing, make nothing of hisself. He just with the fast time. It ain't the world, it's them in the world. He's traveling fast, on fast time. He going and going and going. But before things end up, he going run into something. It's always best to be slow to be sure. That's the way I see it. You don't have success if you're too fast. You can be too fast to learn music, you can be too fast for anything.

Now, you can go out there too fast, too fast. You can get killed out there by being fast; in a hurry, ain't got time to wait, ain't got time for you to get out of the way. He just like a turning wheel all the time. But fastness don't get you much. Steady and peaceful, you get more out of that than you do in being fast. I was raised and taught that. Slow is the way. The farther way around is the nearest way.

Field hollers? Well, I've heard a heap of people sing out in the fields that-a-way, singing different songs, but I haven't heard 'em lately, 'cept by me. Used to holler blues. Mighty near everywhere you went, hear somebody singing the blues in the field. And at night sometime, walking down the road. You don't hear too much of that now. They just changed up. They on this fast time now.

But back there, they used to sing, oh,

different songs. Some sang the blues, some used to give out just church songs. Sing and chopping cotton out in the field, give out hymns. Sing just like they was in church. And some of 'em get on an old mule at night, riding up and down the road, his shirttail hanging out and his cap be out behind. Old mule loping along, and hollering the blues just as loud as you can. Folks would get up and light their lamp and listen at him sing the blues. The old cornfield blues. And they could sing 'em. Used to sing a song: "All right Father, I stretch my hand to Thee." That was a church song. "No other help I know." They sung that.

And some of 'em sang these old songs about:

> Old Blue jumped a rabbit.
> He run him a solid mile.
> The rabbit sat down.
> He cried just like a natural child.

The song what I used to sing plowing in the fields:

> Whoa-whoa-whoa-whoa, boy.
> How can I drive it when I done broke my line?

> Whoa, whoa. Whoa, Nell, whoa.
> Oh, my wheel mule crippled. Whoa, boy, my lead mule blind.
> How can I drive it when I broke my line?
> Whoa, whoa. Whoa-whoa. Whoa, boy.
> Get up in the morning, oh, do like Buddy Brown.
> Oh, going eat my supper, I'm going lay back down.
> Whoa, boy, whoa.

Blues is a company-keeper. Picker can be out there or you can be out there working, in the fields, be lonesome out there working. And them things will run across your mind and you pick it up and go to humming and singing. Your work comes easy to you. You gets pacified. You can work easier that way than you can when just look like you bumbling along, nobody say nothing, ain't mumbling nothing, just off to yourself. Ain't no good. But you get you a song and go to singing, it just comes natural. I get me a song, go to start plowing the field—I don't care how wide, I soon step it. Right to the end and right back, talking and singing, going on about my business. The more I sing, the better I feel. I plow 'em too. I plow mules till they faint.

An old song I used to sing in the fields:
I don't want no woman, boys, if her hair no longer than mine.
Hee, haw—

Oh, I don't want no woman, boys, if her hair no longer'n mine.
Yeah, she give me so much trouble, keep me buying rats all the time.
Whoa! Better gee, mule!—
Yeah, I woke up this morning, um-hum, just about the break of day.
I looked on that pillow, at that rat, where my baby used to lay.
Get back over there, now!—
I don't want no woman—whoa, boy —if her hair ain't no longer than mine.
You know she ain't good for nothing but trouble, she keep me buying rats all the time.

Now, I couldn't all exactly tell where drum music come from. When I was big enough to know it, they was playing it. That's from slavery time, from 'way olden back times. That's when they was playing them drums. Come from old people back playing them drums.

See, there's dances they can do behind them drums and march behind them drums and play behind that they can't do behind a record. Everybody likes the drums. You can name drums and get a bigger crowd with 'em at just a picnic or most any kind of entertainment. That record player ain't nothing if a drum hit out there. That's been ever since I knowed. And when I have come up in the world, myself, I seed people take a drum and play drum. I've seed 'em march along in a wagon, going to play drums. Hear drums for five or six miles. Boom. Boom-boom. Boom-boom . . . "Hey, boys, I hear the drums!" "Picnic over yonder. Let's go there this evening, let's go tonight! Yeah, I'm going find it!" They gone.

They's going find it, too. And when they get there, oh, man, dancing out there, their shirttails hanging out, twisting out there and dancing and Charleston, and doing some of everything. "Hey, boy, play the music!" "Oh Lord, the drum going, I'm going too!" "Play them drums! Hit 'em! Hey, Gabe, come on, play them drums! Hey, man, I *know* Gabe going break 'em up. Come on, Gabe." He said, "Okay, get around, boys, we're going jump awhile. Kill a chicken and churn." That's what they call dancing. Big time. We started to dancing. "All right, boys, we going kill a chicken and churn. We fixing to play them drums for you. We fixing to play 'em." And, man, there'd be some peoples there, too.

So I been seeing 'em and going to picnics and stand and watch 'em and looking at 'em, how they motion and play around. I said, "I'm going do that one day. I believe I can do just what he doing." I started on a tin tub. Beat it with sticks. Take my hand and beat that drum and take me some sticks and went to doing just what the next fellow doing.

Practiced and practiced till I got my right lick. Not just pecking on the drum, you got to play tunes on the drum. That's right. So I learned 'em. I started playing on the tin tub when I was fifteen years old, and when I started playing the drum, I was seventeen.

And I learnt myself to blow the fice [fife]. Myself. That's where I learnt. It was a fellow they called Kid Mavery made a cane. We came out the field on rainy days, we'd go out there to the barn, they'd blow the cane. I'd stand and look at 'em. Well, now his cane had eight holes and I couldn't blow his cane. So I got me a cane and got me a nail. Just a plain cane. Started to boring my holes; I couldn't make none out of that. So I went and got me a thick piece of wire and put it in the stove to burn the holes in there. My mama then come: "Get out of the way, boy! What you doing?" I said, "I'm trying make me a fice." "Oh, you ain't going make you no fice. You don't know how to make a fice." I said, "Mama, I'm going make me a fice. I'm going learn how to blow this cane." I learnt.

Every cane I make, there is not but five holes in it. Nobody blow my cane but me. Most of 'em got six or seven holes, some of 'em got eight. But I can take a five-hole cane and blow mighty near anything anybody blow on it. I tuned it in my tune. Play it a little different than a flute; I ain't never played a flute. The fice, you blows right with your fingers, just like you do organ or piano, same thing. You have to key your cane with your fingers. The fice always been with drums. The fice is for to lead drums. Ever since I was big enough to see the drum, know what a drum was, they was blowing fices and beating drums.

Just like the fice, a person when he starts to playing the drum, you got to pick up some of your own; you can't do like the next fellow on playing drums. You got to learn *yourself*. You can't take a man's hand and just hold his hand and make him play the drum. He got to catch the talent himself. When he catch the slight from his body, from hisself, his learning, he can play it. And I done had many of 'em trying to play my pieces on the drum. He can't play it to save his life. And I can't play his'n. And I've had a many one trying to play on me, ain't beat me yet. Course, I'm still trying to learn. I wants to learn more and more every day.

The funniest thing ever happen to me I can tell you. There once was an old man, name was Son Anderson. He 'ceased that evening. So all of us was down there at his house, sitting down. We was all talking. Foggy and raining that night. They was all talking about

haints. See ghosts, what I mean. Call 'em haints. I told 'em wasn't no such a thing as no haint. I says, "Man, I'll go anywhere I want to go. I ain't scared of nothing. Ain't nothing to bother you. What's there to bother you? Nothing. A guy hit me, that'll hurt me. But a haint ain't going hurt you." I says, "I don't believe in nothing like that." They said, "But some will scare you out of head." I said, "Ain't nothing going scare me out of mine. I ain't scared of nothing. I ain't scared of the foggy night or nothing."

So I left there and came on back. It was foggy and dark that night. When I was walking on back, they was in the house talking and I was listening at them, looking through the window, trying to make it that I hear something. It was a half-grown heifer yearling laying at the gate, but I didn't know it and I was walking along there. Son Anderson was laying in the house dead. The cow was out there by the gate. And I walked right up straddle that thing. And when I walked straddle that gelding, she jumped and she said, "Moo-oo." I said, "Ooh, goddammit! Oh-whoa-oa." When she jumped, I just slapped my hands right around her neck. And she was bucking and hollering, man, and I was hollering too. I didn't know what it was. I know it had done carried me that fast and my foot wasn't touching the ground noway till it throwed me.

In the house I went and, man, everybody in there just hollered and laughed. They forgot about the old man laying there dead. Said, "I run up on a haint out there, boys." They said, "Is you scared?" I said, "No, it didn't scare me. Ain't no such thing as scared." I was too scared to say I was scared.

I was taught all my days, till I got up big enough to know, there's white peoples and there's colored peoples. My mother and my grandfather taught me that. Tells me that white peoples is white peoples and colored peoples is colored peoples. And there's some good white peoples and there's some mean white peoples. And there's some good colored peoples and some mean colored peoples. And honor white and colored regardless of who he is, honor him. And I does that. I don't care who he is.

Mr. Ramus Ringold, Mr. Stone Floyd, Mr. Albert Siles, and Mr. Steve Butler, all them peoples in Panola, just in Como, Mississippi. And I can go their house at night and peck on their door.

"Who is that?"

"Other Turner."

"Okay, come on in. What can I do for you?"

"Well, I needs help, boss man. I done fought it long as I could. I can't see the light."

"What's your trouble?"

"Well, I's needs a little money now, some bills are meeting. I don't want the law on me."

"Okay, come on around. What can I do? Just name it. You have always been good and I don't doubt you. I ain't scared of you. You's a man."

I says, "Thank you." No words 'changed at all—he just give it to me. If I said on a day I'm going pay it, if I can't pay it I'll go back and meet that man and tell him that I can't pay it. When I gets it, I don't stop till I goes to him and pays him off.

And the law can drive up out there and he says, "Other." I says, "Yessir . . . no, sir." Any advice I can talk with him or give him, I give it to him. And I ain't never been arrested but once in my life by a white man. And if a white man have got out the car to arrest me, I say, "Please, sir." And then talk with him awhile. "Why is you doing so and so?" "Well, I just didn't know. I beg your pardon."

Only time I ever been arrested, I was

arrested and put in jail one night. Paid fifteen dollars. For nothing! For nothing. Went to a big party one night, was across over here on the Rafer place. I went there with some boys and boys left there and they left me there. And so I was waiting on them to come back; I was sitting out there on a truck.

And when the laws come in there that night, they started arresting peoples, they throw the light on me. "What you doing sitting out there?" I said, "I was waiting on my men, my boys, what I come here with." "Well, here the boys. Go right there with them." There was some more boys arrested, carrying on, you know. Had done handcuffed them to the door! I went on there and he said, "You stand over there." I stood there. Said, "What were you doing?" I said, "Nothing." Well, they arrested us all and carried us to jail. We stayed there until the next day.

So they went to court and I told 'em, "No, I wasn't doing anything." He said, "Well, if you had've been at home . . ." I said, "Well, that's what my mother told me. In bad company, you will have to pay some money out or either you will get in trouble." So I meant it. And had to pay for my learning. If I'd of been at home that night, I'd been away from there, I wouldn't of had to pay that fifteen dollars.

I didn't do anything, just no more'n follow some boys there and was sitting out there on the truck. They arrested the bunch of 'em, but I was in the bunch and just carried me too. I think that was a dirty deal. Which I know it was. I figured a person going to make you pay something, you be probably done done something or they supposed to fine you for something you did. But if you ain't did anything, well, you just didn't do nothing. But still I was in the racket. When the law got you and he says, "Let's go!" you ain't no pleading to do but just go ahead on.

No, I haven't seed white people being mean to colored people lately, but I have seed it. They arrested this guy one time. Kicked him. They arrested him downtown. They said he was drinking, but the boys said he wasn't drinking. The boy was talking and the sheriff, he was talking. And the boy went to talking, sheriff asked him what was he hollering about. "You talking too loud." And the boy said, "I was just talking." He said, "I ain't drinking." He hauled off and kicked the boy and boy run back and told him, "Don't do that." And the sheriff asked him what did he say, "You black son of a bitch, you!" The sheriff, he hauled off and hit him. Said, "Get in that car!" He got in there. He carried him on and locked him up. I left him in town and come on home. But the next Sunday morning I heard he was out. Some white

man got him out.

The sheriff was Mr. Jim Williams. Mean? He wasn't all that bad, but just

38

a little hot tempered. He had a right smart temper. If he arrested, you couldn't 'fended for yourself at all. Everything he said, it had to be that, then he's ready to kick you or hit you or something. He passed and that ended that. Got a good sheriff now.

But I say we got a little better privilege than used to. It's just good and more better privileges. The white is treating the colored better. They getting together. The white peoples understand the colored and the colored understand the white. You used to didn't catch a white laughing and talking with no colored people, didn't shake hands with 'em. They used to didn't do that. But now, not here but in town on further up in Chicago and all, just laugh and talk, sit down at the table. When I was up there in Chicago one time, I sat down at the table and eat with white people. And they even asked me where did I came from. If you go and

tend to your business and behave and respect and treat peoples right, you'll get help anywhere you go. And my mother and grandfather raised me and taught me that.

And now most every store you go in, you see colored peoples. And then some good as white peoples as I ever met I've shook hands with 'em and they have give me and they have helped me. I wouldn't tell a story. There's some good white people. It really is. And some good colored people.

It used to be a time back that white people would furnish you, on the halfers. It's better now. Every tub sits on its own bottom. If you works, you gets it now. But in them times, if you worked or didn't work, you didn't get it. It went the other way all the time. The man take that book and pencil and sit down and you out there in the field plowing hard, pick cotton and carry it to town, and gin it and bring it on and give it to him. He give you what he want out of it. That's the way it was then, but it ain't now.

I've seed the times, you just dare to be sitting up here on this porch and I'm sitting here . . . you couldn't sit here and talk and I couldn't either. There's a man come in here quick and tell you, "Don't be caught on my place, around my hands, my niggers, no more." That's what he say. That's the reason I say it's better. This is my house. But it used to be in time, that was my house on Mr. Nolah's place. I stayed there long as I going by his temper and what he says and under his roof, that was my house. But if I got out from under the rule, I had to leave there. Leave everything that I had there. The good Master done changed that. I'm paying rent on this house right here. Nobody tell you nothing.

I done forgets now when I got mar-

ried. It's been so long. 'Round '42. I met her at Sisten Hill Church. Standing there with her feets up on the steps, standing there resting, looking. She passed me by, going on.

I says, "Hey, girl!" She looked around. "C'mere." She turned around. I said, "How are you doing?" She said, "I'm all right, how are you?" "All right," I said. "Girl, you looks nice." She said, "Thank you."

I said, "Can I grant your company this evening?" She said, "No." I said, "Why?" She said, "I'm otherwise engaged."

I said, "They told me I'm as good a fish in the sea as has ever been caught out." She said, "Yeah, that's what they say." She couldn't see it like that. "I'm kinda in a hurry. I'm going into church."

I said, "Can I talk to you when you come out?" "I don't know." She went on in, and she came back out. After she

41

came back out, I walked up to her face and started talking to her again.

I said, "Will you grant me Sunday to come to your house?"

"I don't know, I don't know. I'd better not tell you that."

I said, "Girl, I'm seeking and trying to find. I needs a good wife. And I want you to be my wife. Will you be?" She said, "I don't know yet. You asked me too soon."

"Well, will you grant me second Sunday at your house?" She granted me that second Sunday to her house. I said, "Okay, I'll be there. I'm going change your mind. Change in the ocean, change in the deep blue sea, and there'll be a change between you and me."

So, all right, I came down there that Sunday. She sat there in the other room, and she talked and she talked and she talked. Had company. Didn't pay me no attention a'tall, just sitting in there talk-ing. I walked up to the room and spoke, said, "Come on out." After the company left, she came back in there with me. I talked with her a little while. I said, "Well, girl, the next time I see you, you're going to tell me something.

So the next time I went down there, she did. I talked with her. Pretty soon, along come a smile. I said, "That's all right." Just smiled. Said, "You watch what I tell you. Before you done with it, you're going be my wife." She said "How do you know?" I said, "I got a feeling. You're going be my wife." And she is. Ain't she sitting there? She just couldn't out-talk me. She just couldn't do nothing with me. She just give over. Now, she says I'm the best and she don't know what she'd do if I'd leave her.

How'd I know she was the one I wanted so soon? Well, it's a feeling. You can mighty near tell what you all can do. If you got it in you and you believe that and that feeling's in you and she can make up her mind, that's it right there. Just get together.

I'll tell you what it takes to stay together so long. It takes confidence and love. And belief. And that's what I believe in. Can't nobody come tell me nothing on Ada. I got confidence in her. And I can trust her anywhere. That's my belief in it. So she's the same way I. We don't have no argument. We don't fight and squabble and do nothing but just what I say goes and whatever she asks me, I try to fulfill her promise if I can. We go just like two children. Laugh and talk and that's the way we go. And gets along fine too.

Been farming ever since we got married. Four children and two grandchildren living with me—got to do something. I farms it all. Cotton, corn, truck patches, all of that. I rent. Farm for my-

self. It's been going pretty good so far. Ain't having no trouble much nowadays. Thank the Lord for it, and we gets out there and we makes it, together. Makes it so far.

No, I don't get that much, to buy much extra. Sure don't. Ain't got enough territory, enough land to do that. What we do on Christmas? Well, we just goes to town and try to get what desire, what we is able to get for Christmas. Far as our money will let us. If we ain't got no money, we don't get that. If we got money, we gets a little stuff to cook and eat and thanks the Lord we living. Till we can do better. And trying to do better.

I have a little money sometime to get the children some presents. Far as I'm able. Five dollars, six dollars, or seven dollars. I can't get what they want, I have to get far as I'm able, to satisfy them like my mother did me when I was coming up. I'd see them big things. "Son,

you don't want that. Mama ain't able to pay." When she said "Mama ain't able," I was through. I was just as satisfied and just as happy if she bought me a little whistle to blow on or something. I'd put it in my mouth and run around and blow it all day. So I raised my kids the same way. That you ain't able to do, go ahead and make out and thank the Lord for what you is got until you can do better. And ask the Lord to help you. And keep trying to press further. He'll make a way for you.

I'd rather farm than one of these jobs. Sure would. I ain't able to meet these jobs. One thing about it—I'm's a home-raised boy and I didn't get my schooling like I desired. And the way these here jobs is now, I ain't qualified on a whole lot of 'em. You got to just really knows your stuff and in some of these places they don't tell you nothing. You got to go there and read them signs and what the

directions say do, and if you don't do that, you liable to come up blowed up, hand clipped off, or something, you don't know. I lost my schooling by trying to help my mother.

Well, if I couldn't farm, I'd just do the best I could. Find something to make a living out of. Anything to make a living to support my family—besides stealing. I don't steal. Don't want to be put in jail.

I wants the straight way; that's the way I was raised up. I tries to treat people right, treat them as they wish to be treated and that's what I likes. Been that all my days and my record is every way I turn from a baby on up—nothing but good—white and colored. And I don't doubt myself. Anytime I call for favors, white people has walked out and favored me, colored people the same way. So I tries to make a record of that and so I thanks the Lord for as far as I done got

46

up until now. Still praying to press further.

Well, sometime I have the notion to leave Mississippi, but sometime I begin to think I'm doing pretty well here and I decide I'll let well do me. Family here and I was raised up and on a farm all of my days and so far I've made it to here. And I ain't doubting myself. I may have to quit. If I do, I just have nerve enough to believe I can make it.

To my ideas, it's pleasure when my peoples all satisfied and I'm satisfied and I gets what I wanted—well, I don't say get all of what I wanted—gets part of what I wanted, enough to get by on. That's the thrill of it, I think. If a person's family all got the good health and well and his home's comfort, he's satisfied and they's satisfied, that's the joy of it. If they's dissatisfied and you're trying to do and they ain't going be willing to help you and follow you, you're just tormented right there. If you got your family satisfied and they're all pleased, and you's pleased, then everything goes along lovely, I think.

3/ Ain't No Picnic
If You Ain't Got No Drums

The Fourth of July is a time for barbecues and picnics.

L. P. Buford's store, located outside Como on the same dirt road to Other Turner's, supplies most of the area with meat and meal, candy and Cokes, tobacco and gas. "L. P.'s," as the local people call it, is more than a store. It is a gathering place where the men can hang out; it has the region's only baseball field, where families congregate on Sundays; and it serves as the meeting grounds for the area's major social events—picnics and barbecues.

On the morning of the Fourth, the field behind the store must be readied for the weekend's coming festivities. There is a picnic stand—thrown together with slabs of scrap wood many years ago—beneath a large beech tree. Several men and boys who have arrived hours early string lights and shovel up the mule manure deposited since the last barbecue.

A few cars and pickups roll into the hard-packed field around 10:30. A wiry little man, who has been wandering around the premises most of the morning boisterously greeting every newcomer, pokes his head into the window of one. "Well, if it ain't R. L. Burnside. I been looking for you. You remember

me—Little Johnny Woods. I blowed harp with you over at Swanson's picnic Labor Day last year."

"Man, the way you blow harp, ain't no way nobody could forget you," R. L. laughs.

After exchanging a word with all those around, R. L. retrieves his aging, beat-up guitar from the back seat. Johnny grins and rummages through his

pockets for his harmonica. As they stroll toward the picnic stand, some of the men recognize R. L. "There's old R. L. Burnside. I mean he can flat lay down a guitar." "He's a blues singing mothah if ever there was one."

R. L., Johnny, and a few others prop up some Coke crates to sit on. Johnny knocks last night's spit from his harmonica while R. L. tunes his "box." Abruptly, R. L. begins picking and strumming in a driving rhythm. He fires out the words in a rapid chant: *"Poor black Mattie, ain't got no clothes/ Fool got drunk, clothes outdoors."* Johnny's shrill harmonica joins the whang of the guitar and the two seem to converge into one pulsating instrument. A crowd gathers; the picnic is under way.

Some two hundred people have arrived since noon. Mr. Buford's son sells barbecue sandwiches for forty cents, cold drinks for a dime. Many don't eat because of the price, but everyone mingles among the cars to wait for the drums to arrive. Men grab at the women and snigger suggestive comments in their ears, provoking fits of laughter or loud rebukes, or both at once. Whoever can get a dollar goes "out to the cornfield" for a pint of the moonshine whiskey being sold at the shed near the picnic stand. Most are soon rowdily drunk.

"I've got a hundred dollars tonight," one man boasts. "Going gamble it off or drink it off or something. Ain't no nigger here going steal it."

"I'm going mess with some of these women before I leave," another announces loudly.

The owner of the drums, V. O. Beasley, saunters up, makes a fire, and holds the drums over the crackling flames to heat the heads. The fife and drum music of the band, very close to pure West African, is found nowhere else in the United

States. As Other Turner says: "You don't hear drums anywhere but here. That's all, right here. You hear these big bands, these trap drums they plays in these cities. But just for the country, it's all we plays.

"At picnics peoples like the drums the best. It's better to dance, it's more enjoyable, and more pleasure. They get out there and dance and twist behind them and just a pleasure to them. That's why the drums just take the day. Ain't no picnic if you ain't got no drums."

Many cluster around the fire as the rumbling of the bass drum and the rolling rattling of the snares rise above the calls and shrieks of laughter amidst the cars. The musicians silence their drums when they are sure the heads are tight. The shrill whistle of the fife is sounded, its piercing notes cleaving the heavy afternoon air. Soon the drums add a frenzied rhythm to the fife's wailing.

The musicians reel and twist from one end of the field to the other as they play.

Men, women, and children dance. Without moving from where they are, men and women begin to sway their bod-

54

ies to the wild rhythm. Laughing kids leap around and in and out between the drums.

The bass drummer sheds his shirt and soon his back is glistening with sweat. The drunken shouts join with the booming, and the smell of gyrating bodies merges with that of beer and whiskey.

The drums change hands frequently during the day, but the fife blower, so wrapped up in the sounds of his cane that he is almost oblivious to the revel around him, continues without interruption into the night.

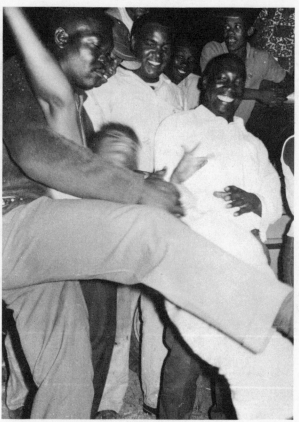

A young woman in a tight white dress jumps in front of him and begins to undulate her hips slowly, working until her whole body is quivering and lurching. The men cheer her on. The fife player cocks his head upward, bending his back toward the ground, and blows the same riff again and again until she

finally collapses into an onlooker's arms. By this time, most of the crowd is

56

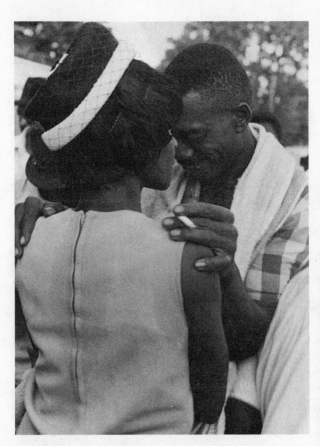

panting, pitching, reeling. For two more days, the frenzy will go on.

4/ *Rosa Lee Hill*

Rosa Lee Hill died in 1968. The following was written before her death.

"How you doing? You know where Rosie Hill stay at? Husband named Ruffan, Ruffan Hill."

"Ruffan Hill, huh? Hey, ain't you Annie Mae, who live over there in Senatobia?"

"No, we done moved from over Senatobia. Live in Como now."

"In town?"

"Uhuh. There along the blacktop out of Como. Third hill past the big highway. Got a mailbox out there in front of the house."

"You know me?"

"I seed you before. I sure done seed you somewhere before."

"My name Mary, Mary Jackson. I been over there where you used to stay at one night. Back about two years ago."

"That's right, I 'member. Say, you know where Rosie Hill stay at?"

"Husband name Ruffan, you say? Ruffan, that preacher over yonder at Hilltop? Name ain't Hill, but it sure is Ruffan."

"No, he ain't no preacher. He a farmer."

"Rosie Hill . . . Oh, yeah, she stay somewhere down the road here a piece. I can tell you near about where she stay

at. You go down this road here and turn back at that big brick house—white folks' house. Go on down the road and pass that church there on the hill. There's some colored folks live there past the church. You turn back and go past a big barn and a burnt-out house. Ask any of them colored people along there where Rosie Hill stay at. Anybody can tell you."

The road back to Rosa Lee's house is not really a road at all, only two rutted lanes through the fields. The modicum of gravel usually peppered over Mississippi dirt roads is missing. High weeds and grass that brush lightly against the underside of the car grow unhindered between the deep ruts.

"Get out, y'all," she calls out the usual Mississippi greeting as a familiar car drives up.

"Let me go in and get out of these rags. I look like a big black bear," she says, laughing heartily as always.

A few years ago Rosa Lee's house was destroyed by fire, and she was forced to move into the little weather-beaten shack where she now lives. The roof of the front porch sags to the point that visitors must bend double to pass under. No trees give protection from the afternoon sun, but because of the light breezes from over the hill, it is the coolest place to be for miles around.

Rosa Lee's father Sid Hemphill was

the most popular musician in the Senatobia area for years before his death in 1961. His first love was the fiddle, but he also played the drums, guitar, fife, quills, and harmonica. The entire Hemphill family were good musicians, but most of them "just didn't feel like playing no more" when Sid died.

Rosa Lee stopped playing guitar when he died but has recently taken it up again. She picks the bass strings firmly, making them "say what she's saying,"

and sings out in a rich, pure voice. Rosa Lee, more than anyone else in the family, always followed her father in his love of music.

You know, I done forgot the year I was born in. See, I'm just fifty-six years old right now. And I'll be fifty-seven the twenty-fourth of next month. I was born in Panola County, right south of here. Como. That's where I was born at.

My daddy's name Sid Hemphill. That was his name. His father's name Doc Hemphill. That's what he was named.

My father was just a musician— straight musician. Well, see, my father, when he was a boy, he got his eyes, you know, one of his eyes knocked out and that put the other one out. And he blacksmithed it—make chairs, shoes, baskets —and a musician, he was just a straight musician.

Played violin, guitar, drums, mandolin, banjo, harp. He just play any kind of music you can—he just a straight musician. His own daddy was a musician. Played a violin like my daddy. Play anything that he play. He played till he was seventy years old.

My daddy played everywhere. Down here at the Delta, up here in the hills, and play in Memphis—just everywhere. Play for white till ten o'clock and then play for colored till twelve at night. And he play music from Monday till Monday again.

He played down here at Sardis, between Sardis and Como. They paid him thirty dollars—the tips that they take up with the hat. Played every Wednesday night. Playing for Mr. Fowler Mac-Arthur. He was running to be the sheriff, the high sheriff. He'd have a speech, you know, and he'd play for him.

And he played with the shows, played for circus shows and this here Rabbit Foot Shows when I got big enough to know him. They danced and had animals, you know. The ladies danced and then the mens and children all was dancing. They had good shows. On wagons. It looked like a big green wagon with them there big elephants, and they had tents put up. They'd sell candy and apples and then dolls and balls and just everything.

They played in towns, Alabama and in Memphis and Crenshaw and just every way. They traveled, you know. And they was nice shows, too, and had good music. Lots of musicians there, but they claimed my daddy was the best one there, him and his boys. We girls wasn't big enough to play then. He had a whole band; I think it was six of them. They had violin, guitar, horns, drums, pans, and bones. Those trap drums. You hit them and them bones do like that, you know. And them pans, they had all of them. They had them slide horns and them there little old jazz horns you put in your mouth. They had them too.

He didn't pick the guitar with one hand. He picked it with both. Had all ten fingers going at once. He could throw it way out in front of him and it didn't never stop saying what he wanted it to. Could put the fiddle behind his back and under his leg and the whole time he kept playing it.

Played those old songs. The "Old Hen Cackle" and "Arkansas Travel" and the "Carrie Song." He made them songs up. "The War Song" had twenty-one verses in it, and the "Carrie Song," it had twenty-one. Just made 'em up about things around.

I felt like my father—well, he was just real good. We didn't never had to do anything, farm or anything, when my daddy was living. He just made his living playing music and teaching us. See, after we

growed up, he didn't have to get nobody else, just his three children.

I lived there where I was born at until I was about ten years old. And I was playing music then. Started playing music when I about between seven and eight years old. 'Cause when I was ten I was playing for dances. Playing guitar. My daddy learned me. I would sit up when he go off to play at night and tell 'im to tune it up, you know. I'd meet him at the door and take it and go to playing. I'd play till I get sleepy.

When I was ten, moved down here to Crenshaw, stayed there for two years. That's where I stay when my mother 'ceaseded. I was going to school then. I went to school till I was twelve years old. It was just a large room, that's all it was. You see, in them times peoples wasn't able to build a school and, see, we had to buy books in them times. And you don't get much education when you have to

63

buy books 'cause people ain't able to buy. My daddy had to buy my books.

It was a man teacher there, name was Bob Ellis. He was a good teacher, yessir, and a mean teacher too. He like to whip you. Look like he whip you too much. Whipped us with a switch. Whip you if you didn't know that lesson. He was 'bout tall as my husband there and wasn't no little man and he would natural whip you. He wouldn't promise to you, he'd whip you.

I learned a little there as far as my daddy was able to buy my books, you know. See, my daddy wasn't able to buy the books I called for and that cut me off. I was about twelve when I finished school, 'cause I didn't have no books. Then I went straight playing music then. I cried about my books. They wouldn't give 'em to you then; no, sir, you had to go buy them books.

When I was about twelve we left Cren-shaw and moved to Sardis there on Front Street and put us up a restaurant and we played there. I stood on a little block and sold pies. Ten cents a pie. My auntie made the pies. I wasn't big enough to cook them, but I could sell 'em. To the men that worked there in the mill there in Mr. Carrie's there in Sardis. My daddy was playing there at the cafe. We had a nice place there. They had the cafe on the front and we had a hairdresser in the next room. We made good money. Right there in Sardis. We had the cafe about two years.

We left then and went back to Cren-shaw and my daddy, he put up a shoe shop. Went to working on shoes and chairs and play music at night and work at the shop in the daytime.

And we play music at night. All of us could play then. He played the violin and I played the guitar and my baby sis-ter played the bass violin—she was 'round about nine then. She could play it, too. Play it with the bow and then put the bow down and then she would pick it. That sound good, picking, don't it. I can play a bass violin now. I love to play. Everybody in my family played. My mother, my daddy, my auntie, and my grandpa played, all my cousins and sisters played. The whole Hemphill band played music—all of 'em.

Any way we go, this-a-way, go east, south, west, any way, they hear tell of Rosie. Now when I was little I played everywhere. I play for the white, I play for the colored, I play for anybody that want me to play. And I loved it because I was young, you know, and I loved to play music.

Even the little youngsters could sing then. I used to could really sing. I used to stand on my daddy's chair and bring the tears from the older people's eyes 'cause I could sing. I had a good voice and I

wouldn't shake. I done got older now, but I really used to sing. That's all I used to do is sing, pick guitar, and play music.

We played all kinds of music then. We played the blues, them that want to hear it, and them what liked church songs, we'd play them. Just like we'd go to their house, they wanted blues, we'd play it. And if we go to white people's house, they wanted waltzes, fox trots, we'd play that for them. And then we'd go to older people's house, they wanted church songs, well, all of us would get together and sing and play that. They'd be happy, shouting it. Yes, sir, that's the truth. They'd be happy and shouting and crying.

I likes all the music. I gets worried sometimes, you know, and I sing the blues, it makes me feel better. That gives my mind ease. Makes me rest. When I get worried, that'll sing them

65

worried blues away from you.

But the blues, you know, is for the bad man and the church songs for the Lord.

That'll carry you the other way, singing the blues. I just sing 'em, you know. See, that ain't from my heart, I just sing that from my mouth. Then ask the Lord to forgive me.

You want the truth from me? When I'm real happy, really happy? Well, that's when the spirit hit me, when I'm in the church.

That was about my happiest memory when a kid. When I got up some size, I can remember when I 'fessed religion I was glad. Now that was the best days, when I 'fessed religion. I was seventeen years old then. Ooh, just looked like everything was new. I was just as light, looked like. I don't know when I left the bench. And looked like everything was new to me. I ain't never felt that-a-way before.

That's the reason I said all this blues is from my mouth. It ain't from my heart. 'Cause I know I been changed. I have fun, you know. That ain't to make you pleasure less, you know, when you 'fess religion. You can ask the Lord to forgive you for that. He'll do it.

How do you feel when the spirit hits you? Well, it hits you right in there. Make you feel good. But it don't last long, it don't drive you crazy. You just feel good. Sometimes you shout and sometimes you just cry. And you be right light.

I know I was at the church, the spirit hit me once—my husband was right there. And a man was squatting out there in the church and the spirit hit me. I just stepped on over him and went on up to the pulpit. But, really, I didn't see him. When I come back, my husband told me, said, "You just walked all over that man." I said, "I didn't see him." But, see, I was just happy, you know. I just light. Just went on over them benches, just went on about my business. Think-

ing about the Lord and my soul is happy. I believe Jesus is with me. Least I know He is.

Now, right here at home I can get to singing a good hymn or singing a good song or even just imagining it in my mind, that-a-way, and I go to crying. But see, the spirit has got to be in there for me to do that. I can just get to singing here at home. No longer than this morning when I was making my bread up, I was singing that song about "When they crucify my Lord" and that just hit me. And I couldn't move! I was standing there with my hands up that-a-way. And this little child come there, she said, "Go ahead on." I just got happy. I couldn't get to go to church, I went to singing. And that felt good. Oh, I know I been changed. I know that.

Well, I played music slam on up till I was married. I married in '41.

Married at the preacher's house. We

had a nice time at the wedding—eating, drinking, and they was throwing rice on us. And when my husband went to kiss me, another person kissed me—another man. I knowed it wasn't him, I backed back. I knowed at that time that'll be about the first kiss my husband would give me and so I backed back, so he wouldn't get mad. I say they did that for a big joke.

We never did have no kids. That little girl was give to me. First cousin's girl. Went out of her head, she had thirteen children, and who give Georgia to me. She was just a little old thing when I got her. She done gotten fatter since she live with me. Yes, sir. She was four years old when I got her; she ten now.

When I got married, see, Ruffan a farmer and that was the first farming I ever done. Now, it look like we just ain't making nothing farming. It's gotten bad for us.

When I was growing up, you take in them times, see, you raise your own cows, hogs, chickens, and you wouldn't have anything to buy except just a little sugar and coffee, 'cause you raise your bread when you raise your corn. Well, you do pretty good in them times. But now you have to buy everything and it looks like the sharecroppers poor now, 'cause we have to buy everything. 'Cause we ain't raising like us been doing. Things sure have gotten worse for us.

Started picking cotton this year in October and picked on up, well, I reckon till February. We just got through in February. And we had a hard time gathering it in and didn't get nothing out of the crop after gathering it. The price of it was cheap and then, you know, making the crop was expensive. Poison, fertilizer, you know, taking that up. And the crops was cheap. Made four bale. Come out way behind. Didn't come out with

nary'n a nickel. We didn't pay our debts. Didn't get anything but a balance due. The crop was short. And it just didn't reach it. Work that many months and on the end don't get anything and all your labor be under there.

The man who owns this place furnished us. Twenty-five dollars a month. That's what he furnished us a month— twenty-five dollars. Charged ten cents interest on the dollar. Had to pay him that out of the cotton crop. Sure did.

See, us wasn't paying rent when we was making the crop. We don't pay then. But when us ain't farming we have to pay ten dollars a month for this house. And we don't get no twenty-five dollars a month when we ain't farming. That's on our crop.

I ain't got no money to live off of now, no more than what this man up here give Ruffan to feed his cows for him. Well, Ruffan take that. And buys a little something and pay our light bill.

Ruffan: Seem like I'm going have to try to go down to public work now. Ain't nothing in farming. They won't give you nothing for it, for your crops. The people done quit farming. They gone into day working. Them around here used to farm, biggest ones is day working now. Mighty few colored peoples farm. I'm the onliest man, me and that colored man over yonder—we the only two people on this place. But he done quit now, and ain't no one on this place farm but me. Everybody say ain't nothing in no crops. Tell a person now you're farming, he'll tell you in a minute you ain't doing nothing, and the way it's running, you're not.

I just feel like I gotta quit farming. I love to farm but farming got so expensive, don't make no crop, ain't getting anything out of it. So I have to quit. I love to farm, sure 'nough. And I hate to quit farming. But I have to quit because I not making a living out of it. And I have to hunt me a job that I can make a living out of. Sometime, you ain't getting nothing, try something else.

70

Rosa Lee: How many meals do we eat a day? Well, sometimes one and sometimes nary'n. You know you can train yourself any way you want. You can train yourself to eat three meals a day and you can train yourself just to eat one a day. Wait till you get hungry and eat if you ain't got nothing to cook next time. You know. I usually scratch something to give this little girl. She going to school. Ruffan works every day and only eat one meal and that's at night. When he come home from work. He don't eat nothing through the day.

Yes, I've thought about leaving Mississippi. I started to leave once before. Yes, I would leave Mississippi in a minute. Anywhere I could live and make a living, whether I like it or not, I would just stay there. Whether I liked or whether not, if I be making a living, I'm satisfied and I'm happy. If I do better than I'm doing here in the North, I would go North. But this is my home, Mississippi, and if I'd do better in the North, I would go North and buy me a home in the North.

It was in '61, when my daddy 'ceaseded, that I thought about leaving before. I was going up yonder with my sister to Minnesota. That's where I was going, on with her. Well, my husband, he had a sister down here and she didn't want him to go. So, you know, a man and a wife should be as one, and he wanted to stay and I stayed on with him. My sister, she was married and she had children in the North to take care of her, but I didn't have no kids up there to help me. And I just stayed where my husband was— here.

If I had one wish, it'd be for enough money to get me a home to live in and be happy long as I live. Yessir, I would really be proud if I could own one, a house to live in. I really needs one of 'em. I's outdoors now, just in a shelter. Sure is. I thinks about it and speaks about it mighty near every day.

Now I had another house but it burnt down last year. And I just did get out. I give that up 'cause when my husband woke me up, the house was full of smoke. And he called me, said, "Get up, Rose, your house is falling in."

And I said, "Where the baby?"

He said, "I got her."

I said, "We'll all hold to each other. I know where the door is." And I just stooped over and got the door. I said, "Now, y'all hold to me. When I jump out, y'all come on, 'cause it going collapse when the wind hit it."

So I opened the door and we all jumped out at the same time. And it just collapsed.

And everything I had was in there. I knew I could get most things, but I couldn't get me another Rosa. I thanked the Lord for saving us all and didn't burn us up. We didn't get burnt, didn't go back in there for nothing. And everything I had was in there. All my food and furniture, all my money, but my life wasn't in there. And I thanked Him for that. I could've not woke up and all three of us could've got burnt up. Yes, sir, I sure thank Him for that. I thank Him for that.

My house was burnt up on the sixth

of January in 1966. They put it up in Senatobia on the broadcast station. The man what broadcast up there, he came there just about the time it had felled and he didn't know our names, took our names, and he put it on the air. And they gave us everything y'all see in this house, 'cause we didn't have any money or anything to buy anything with. When your house get burnt down and everything you got get burnt up in it, you have a pretty tough time. And we didn't know too many peoples when we moved up in here, see. But they was nice to us, white and colored. Gave us clothes to put on. We didn't have anything but what we run out of the house with. All the rest was burnt up. That's the first time I ever been burnt out in my life.

I was scared when my house burnt down. And then there was another time I was really scared. This here twister come along. When the clouds get all made up like an ice cream cone—well, it will have a tail to it hanging down that-a-way. Well, it will come on down. And that cloud just rolling. And just make music. I'll tell you when there's going be one—in the daytime it will get black dark; you have to pull your lights on. Well, you can look out.

Well, this time this here twister come along. Me and my Aunt Curley was standing outdoors and here it came rolling, black. And I had my arms folded, standing in the door. And I said, "Lord, don't let this storm come. Please turn that storm." And I could hear the people hollering up in the air. See, they was up in the air. They was in the storm hollering "Lord, have mercy." The storm had 'em, you know, toting them.

And it just went down the wire fence, just taking them posts up. And the wind just hit the house every now and then. And I never did shut my doors or noth-

73

ing. I just trust in the Lord. It just angled when I had my arms folded that-a-way. I said, "Lord, please don't let that storm come up that hill rolling and kill Rosie. Please, Lord!" And my auntie, she spoke, we was praying.

It turned. Turned just as good and went on up that fence and took up them there barntops. And come on up here right across over to that sanctified church. There was a widow lady and her childrens there. It took the top off of their house and just left them sitting there.

I just knowed the Lord heard me 'cause I was really scared. That was a bad storm that day. It went all the way around. That's the reason I knowed that the Lord heard me. I was scared but he heard me. 'Cause it sure turned. I was 'bout as scared then as when we got burnt out.

I was really sad when my house

burned down. And I'll be sad when, you know, something happens in the family or either I can't get hold of nothing. I'll be real sad then. And sorry too. If something happens bad in the family, well, I'll be real sad then.

But through life I stay happy. Hardly ever I feels sad. I'm merry. I stay happy.

The harder it get with me, the higher I hold my head. See, I don't hold my head down and just grieve, I hold my head up. And that makes me feel better. See, if you fall, don't wallow, get up. And hold your head up. When it's hard for you, look up. Don't look down, look up. That's a good way to be, ain't it?

5/ *Jessie Mae Brooks*

Jessie Mae Brooks, Rosa Lee's niece, lives about a quarter of a mile over the hill from Rosa Lee. Her house lies to the side of a large meadow of tiny yellow flowers that grow wild in the hill country. Her boyfriend's white pickup truck is often parked inside the heavy wooden gate and barbed-wire fence enclosing the house.

A good-looking woman, she usually changes into a shapely dress with bright green or yellow spangles, a long black wig, and a rhinestone tiara when visitors drop by. "Primping like a Hemphill," Rosa Lee says. And she "always likes to give something to eat to someone what comes" to her house. A special visitor might get a meal of fried chicken, honey, vienna sausages, and peanut butter, even if she has to go without food for a couple of days to buy it.

She misses her grandfather Sid Hemphill and the times when she would join the Hemphill band on guitar or bass drum at parties and picnics. Today, she finds an outlet for her music at churches in the area. At the end of services, cries of "Amen" and "Tell the truth, girl" rise from the congregation when she sings her own songs showing Christ in their everyday experiences:

Don't let Him catch you in the

77

whiskey store,
Said He was coming, you'll
    never know.
I want to be ready when Jesus
    comes.

Still young, but disillusioned with life in Mississippi, she is torn between venturing North and remaining where her roots and friends are.

78

I'm thirty-seven. I don't know exactly what year it was I was born in. I was born in Panola. Wasn't too far out from Como. He farmed, my father. After him and my mother separated, me and my mother just lived together. They separated when I was about three or four years old.

My mother, she farmed one or two years, and then she started cooking for white peoples all the time. She cooked at Miss Maygay's about four or five years. I was too small to remember the others, but she worked for the white peoples all the time. She knitted, worked in the field, you know. Too much. Just wasn't nobody but her and I didn't have no daddy, so we just stuck together till she left me. When she passed, I didn't have nothing else left. She been dead ten years ago. This year she'll be dead ten years.

She didn't get paid much for cooking. She didn't get anything that much. You know, they'd give her little something and the rest of it would be clothes for me, you know, something for her, something like that. She didn't get no money too much. All they would give her just something like what they didn't need. When I got large enough to know better, I tried to tell her better—that she didn't have to work for me for no clothes and things. I had that many clothes, and she work and they would give her, you know, frigidaire, or stove, or something, and then a little money.

Now my mother got married twice after her and my father separated. And she left both of them. And she died ten years ago after she had an operation, but my second stepfather, he was the real cause of it. Of her dying. Fighting her and everything.

Just like I was telling you about my auntie in the North what I called last night and she said she's got this tumor.

And her husband is the one who give her that tumor. She got this tumor fighting with her husband. It was in '40-something. They was fussing as a woman usually will do a man when he go out and stay all night long. And so they just got arguing and he jumped on her and hit her with something. He go out with other women and so she was fussing and that make him fight then. And so he had to hit her to keep her from almost killing him. And that's what give her this tumor.

Now it was the same with my mother. I was three or four when she married my first stepfather. When she married the other one, I was fifteen. The first one, his name was John Henry Ramsey, and we stayed over here from Como on Mr. Guy Watson's place at the time. And so the way they separated . . . she went over to this house and he was over there with this lady and they were sitting there playing cards and the lady was sitting in his lap. And so Mother had me by the hand and it was dribbling rain and we was standing out there. And the window pane was out and the curtain would blow up, you know. And so she just looked through the window when the curtain would blow up and see my stepdaddy sitting there playing cards with the lady in his lap. When the wind would blow the curtain back, she would ask me who was that. And I'd see him and I'd say, "That's Daddy . . ." And I was four years old.

So when the card game broke up, she went 'round there. And when they opened the door, she walked in there and they ran out in this field across from that house and he hit her with a piece of stove, you know, a four-cornered stove piece. He throwed it back. She was in the dark, she couldn't see him, and I was holding on to her arm, and he throwed

it back and hit her and broke her arm in two places. I just went to hollering and saying, "C'mon, Mama; c'mon, Mama."

Mama was wearing a raincoat and her arm had done swole up so big that when the doctor got there, he had to cut that raincoat off her arm. He put a brace on it. And so she told my daddy, "When the doctor takes this brace off me, you better be gone because I'm going kill you." And so my stepdaddy knew she meant that and he went to the fields and he come back, and that was the day the doctor 'sposed to come and take the brace off. He said, "How you feel?" She said, "Feel fine but I'll feel better once the doctor gets this brace off." He says, "Well, I'm gone." And she said, "You better be gone."

And so he walked on out and went up the road. I went to the door and I told him, I said, "When I get grown"—the last thing I was saying as fur as I could

see him—"When I get grown, get up a big girl, I'm going kill you myself, wherever I see you at."

I was fifteen when she married my next stepdaddy. So him and her used to fight the same way. I never lived with her too much, with the last one she had. Because he didn't want me to live with 'em, he was so mean, you know, to me. So I went to Memphis and stayed. And I'd come back to see her and leave again. And when I was up there, he would fight her and she had been operated on and this is what kilt her. He would jump on her and when he would jump on her, this is the first place he would hit her. He'd kick her in the stomach and that what kilt her. Fighting and kicking her in the stomach.

That's why I say I just don't want to marry. Not right now. 'Cause of just fighting with these men. I just don't want to fight with 'em, 'cause I wouldn't let nary'n one of 'em fight me.

I want one so old that he'll just sit over there in that corner and I would

81

just tote his food to him and tend to him and he couldn't fight me. That's about the only way I'll get married, is marry one that's old. To keep from fighting with one, I wouldn't mind being married to one that old. But if I could get one that's young and he wouldn't fight, I'd be glad to get married tomorrow. But if he want to fight, he have to be by hisself.

Now, I was married. Once. And me and my husband separated. Got married in '52. So we stayed together about a year. But he wanted to fight and he wanted to run around and I just let him go.

I met him at a drive-in when I was living in Memphis. We went to a club to eat sandwiches. And then he got in his car and I got in my car and we was sitting side by side. So he said, "How 'bout me trailing you home?" I said, "Okay, that's a good deal." So he trailed me on the house. So we sat there in the drive

and talked till about 10:30. And he carried me to the movie the next couple of nights, and that Sunday we went to church together. And that was the day, when we went to church together . . . I seed he liked church and I like the church, so I thought I was getting myself somebody. Somebody, you know, who wanted to do right and didn't want to fight. I thought I had got somebody who wanted to have something, I mean that's what I married for.

At first, oh, it was lovely; we was so lovely. I was working when we first married and so he stopped me from working and he was working two jobs. And we doing fine.

Now I wasn't the cause of us separating, I'd say. It was mostly him wanting to fight after we moved. And we moved in a apartment with a lady what wasn't married and they started to going together and then I left him. That's what

separated us. It was mainly the woman. I just left him on account of that, be-

cause if he started with one, he going keep it up with another one and then I was going to be in trouble 'cause I would've hurt him or something. So I let him go.

And I've been single ever since. And I don't want to tie up with another June bug. A June bug—they wants to fight all the time. And so, I don't like fighting. I like to marry and have something and live together for something. Have a happy home, not no home that you got to raise sand all the time.

I've thought about getting married since then, but I haven't found anyone yet. Least I haven't trusted nobody. I hadn't trusted anybody yet. I'm scared to trust 'em. But sooner or later, I got to trust somebody. Of course, maybe I could marry twenty and they all going court, but I mean, after all, courting in a way that I wouldn't know nothing about it. Not right in the house with me or right around me. If he court all across town, that would be all right. Just so I wouldn't know anything about it and he would take care of me and take care of home.

So, anyway, after my mother left my second stepfather, I came down here and stayed with her. I stayed two years before she got sick. And I couldn't never leave to save my life. Every time I'd try to leave, I wouldn't get enough money, and if I got enough money, I would spend some of it. And I just couldn't get away. I done that for two years. Couldn't get away from her.

And so, one night I was laying down, and she was in the room and I was in the other. I was just looking at the moon shining. And I said to myself, I said, "Why is it I can't leave home this time when I been leaving all the time—left 'fore I was grown—but I can't leave now? And every time I would come I could leave." So I said, "Lord, why can't I leave now?" And it's just something that come to me and told me: "You just stay with Mother long as you can, 'cause she won't be with you no long time."

And sure enough, she got sick. She got sick and I stayed with her then a year. I carry her everywhere—Memphis and everywhere—to the hospitals and things. Nobody wanted her but me, but I stuck with her. I lift her around, and she weighed 150, and I lift her around, and I wasn't weighing 100 hardly. But that was my mother and I loved her.

Took her to the hospital in Memphis. The doctor operated on her. He asked me could he operate on her. I told him, if he thought he could get her well or make her better he could operate on her. But now he knowed he wasn't going to make her better and he didn't have no business cutting her. See, I could've got money out of that. I could've had sued that hospital but I didn't. 'Cause, see, when I told about if he couldn't get her well, then don't operate, and he went and cut her anyway and that's what killed her. She hadn't even fell off or nothing. She hadn't lose nary'n a pound. And I kept on telling him, I kept asking him all the time, would it do her any good. And he kept telling me he didn't know. Said they take X-ray pictures that tall a stack of 'em and they couldn't see nothing wrong with her. Well, if he didn't see nothing inside her wrong with her, reckon why did they cut on her?

And after they cut on her, she just went on down. And they put her on that diet and she couldn't eat nothing and she just went on down—just where she couldn't do nothing. And then I brought her back home. And see, here what I could've sued 'em about—they just burnt her up. See, it wasn't the cutting all by itself, but it was them 'lectric treatment they were giving her. Today they would

put it here, you know, put her on that table and put that old 'lectric thing down on her stomach; tomorrow they put it down on her back. You know, just cooked her lungs and everything all up that way. She just cooked up inside. See, they didn't know what the matter with her and they just cooked her up like that. My mama. Sure did.

I was two years old when I got interested in music. I used to just get up anywhere. I didn't care if it was church songs, dancing, singing. When I was little, two years old, I used to dance. I win the prize everywhere in Mississippi that I would dance. I would win the prize at the show. They give shows. Down here at Miss Maygay's store—she give a show down there for the peoples to dance, you know. So a colored guy—he was a grown man; I was about seven then . . . the tap dance. She wanted the tap dance. So he was tap dancing. And I looked at him dancing. Then they called me up there. I was a little old girl. I was 'shamed that night—I don't know why I was 'shamed. I was 'shamed 'cause he was a man and I was just a little girl, I guess. But if he had been a child like me, I would have been tough. When I got up there I said, "Well, I'm going dance anyway." So I went on and just tap danced till I couldn't even walk hardly. I beat him, though. He could do it, but I beat him.

I win that prize. I win all the money and I had all the money them folk could throw up there. And Miss Maygay, she gave me a case of Cokes and I don't know how much cloth. You know, she had a store right there. How much cloth she give my mother! Beautiful, to make me all kinds of dresses and shoes—she give me all that stuff. 'Cause I could dance so good and beat that man dancing and I wasn't nothing but a little old

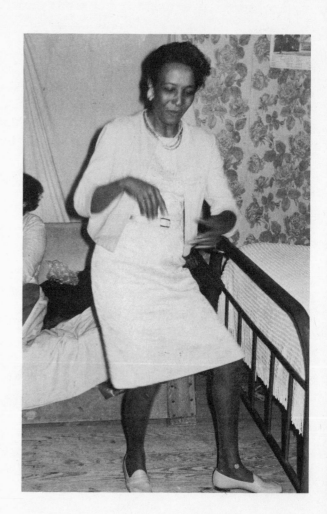

girl. The man come shook hands with me, said I was the best. He said, "I have to give it to you, you were the best." So I winned that one.

I done win so many prizes so many places. For playing the drums. Just this year, in July, down here at this picnic for Mose Swanson. Was five men down there beating the drum, and I took and beat the drum and winned the prize for that.

I started playing the guitar when I was nine. My granddaddy Sid Hemphill, he would tune it for me. When I got the guitar, I'd go out, 'way out from the house, by myself. And when I get out there, all I do is ask my granddaddy to tune it for me. You see, I couldn't catch on how to tune it, but I could pick it. So my granddaddy tuned it for me and I took the guitar and went on out from the house.

I'd sit out there and I pick it and I'd pick and sing. I wouldn't pick nothing if I wasn't singing. And anything I'd sing, I'd try to make the strings say what I say. That what my granddaddy taught me. If the strings don't say what I say, I wasn't picking what I sing. You'd be singing one thing and picking another. So I went on and went to picking what I sing.

And then I learned how to blow the harp. I quit blowing it, it took so much wind. When I started beating drums, that was . . . oh, I was, say nine or ten, like that. I was learning it all at the same time. Drums, guitar. I'd just go in the room and then try all of 'em.

I learned how to beat the drums, and I would take the drums when they go off. When they would leave home, I'd take 'em and hook 'em up, you know, on the porch rafter and get up on a chair, see. I wasn't tall enough to reach 'em, I'd get up in a chair. I'd get up and I'd take that stick and I'd beat that drum till the time went along. And there'd be so many cars out there in that road— thought it was a picnic, you know. And they'd be just jumping up in the yard and driving up there and parking 'side the road.

And they'd say, "Where your grand-daddy?"

And I'd say, "Granddaddy not here. Ain't nobody here but me."

They say, "You the one beating them drums?"

I say, "Yes, sir!" That what I say, you know, 'cause there be all of 'em. There be white and colored be just stopped and think it's Sid Hemphill, you see. 'Cause they know him. And it wouldn't be nobody but little old me up there in that chair beating that drum down.

Let's see what else I learned. Learned how to play piano, organ, and I played church songs mostly on them. Or boogie or something. I didn't know how to play no blues on them too much. Then I learned how to play the tambourine. You know you play tambourine in sanctified. Well, Granddaddy would play church songs and I'd play tambourine for him. I played the tambourine on my hand, on my elbow, on my knee, on my toe, and on my head. Played it all the way over me. And I winned the prize off of that. That was in Crenshaw, Mississippi. We played at churches for them peoples. So I just played tambourine. I wasn't 'shamed of nobody. I'd just play and I wasn't as big as nothing. I wasn't 'shamed of no grown folks, wasn't 'shamed of white. I'd just get up in front of them and play and win all that money. I just wanted to win me some money. That's what I want. Buy me big things.

Now everytime I just give up on music or give up trying to think up songs, it just come right back in my mind again.

One Sunday I came out here in the swing and I was sitting out here, and I said, "I'm going to church Sunday and I'm going think me up something to sing." I went in there and got the Bible and read one verse out of that. And so I took that one verse and just put me some more to it and made me a good church song. And I went to church that Sunday evening and I sung it on that program. Just get a verse and I thinks of mine. I make up the tune and when I think it's all right, then I go sing it somewhere, in some church. And peoples like it.

Now I know you done heard this song, "There's Going To Be a Fire Burning One Day You Can't Put Out." Now I was the first little old girl that put that song out. I was about eleven or twelve. It just come to me, and I was outdoors. Me and my granddaddy was at home and I was out on the porch washing—when I'm washing I always find some song to sing—and so that song just come to me like that. And every time I say one verse, another verse would come up and I just say that one.

So my granddaddy was sitting in the house and he came and stood in the door and he said, "Baby . . ." I said, "Sir?" He said, "Where'd you get that little song from?" I said, "I don't know, sir, it just come to me and I just started singing it."

He said, "You almost through washing?" I said, "Yessir." He said, "Well, come on, let's see can we play that. You done thought up something good."

And I went in the house and he tuned his fiddle up, and I took the guitar and he tuned it up for me and I went to singing it and picking it on the guitar.

Now, I was the first little girl to sing that. But some grown peoples took it and changed some verses and made some money off it. And I was the one that

89

thought of that song. And my grand-daddy played it on his fiddle and I picked it on the guitar, with the clothes in the tub.

Now, Uncle Sid, he wrote all his own songs. Like something that would happen. Just like something go on in town or someplace and he would hear of it and he would just take everything that happened, he would take that and make a song up out of it. And he would make up blues, like that one Aunt Rosa sang about "Mama in the kitchen cooking pork and beans/ Daddy in the ocean running submarines." He made that up.

He never could see good. He wanted to go to school, but it hit him in the eye. He went to work in the blacksmith shop and the man, the doctor, told him, "Don't work over the heat 'cause it will affect the other eye." And that made cataracts come on his good eye and that made him couldn't see, you know.

But he could make anything. He made chairs, he made me a drum, he made me a bedroom suit and a poster bed, he could make that. He'd just get the stuff and he'd feel it and take his tools—he had all kinds of tools—and he'd just make those things. He made me a fiddle like his fiddle, and 'fore he died, he was fixing to make me a guitar. Anything I'd tell him I wanted, he'd do it. Made me a guitar. He didn't have it together, you know. He had done shaped it. But he didn't finish it. After that, I didn't have nobody to make me nothing else. So I was just lost from then.

Oh, I was shouting awhile today. That was 'cause of me thinking about my auntie having that tumor. When your burden get heavy, you're supposed to pray and shout and praise God in your own way at home. And wasn't nobody here but me and whenever I feel like praising God I just go to praying and read my Bible and I'm just happy as I can be. I enjoy it, I be just "Thank you, Jesus! Thank you, Jesus!" I'll be as happy as I can be. And you can hear me from here to the road. I just don't be caring who hearing me right then. I really feel happy. I sure do.

And so I prayed for my auntie today that the Lord will heal her. After I prayed for the Lord to heal her, I read the verse of James in the Bible where it says, "Is there any sickness among you? To call for the elders of the church. Let them pray over you and annoint you with oil in the name of the Lord." I read that. And I read, "The prayers of faith will save the sick." And when I prayed, I asked the Lord if he had healed my auntie to show me some way or 'nother that he had healed her, and I just went out of that chair, just like that, and I was shouting and happy.

It's lonesome here by myself. Ooh, nobody to say something to and these mosquitoes and this bird. I reckon that by you having your car lights on, it's scaring the birds that hollers all the time. But he hollers all night and I wish he would go away. And living here in the dark . . . I just knew I didn't have the money to get the lights turned on, so I just wait until I can get it.

Hard to be a woman living alone? Wooh-wee, it's natural just miserable. It's miserable to live alone by yourself. You can think of so many things just laying woke at night, so many things you can think of. You just be thinking you could marry . . . or I would marry . . . or I would get somebody but he might be this and he might be that. You would leave and go to another place . . . you might not do so good there. And it's just so many problems you have to think of. Most of the time you already have

to . . . there nobody there. Sometime you wants to go somewhere . . . nobody to take you nowhere. Sometime you would say, "I would get up and fix me so-and-so," some food, but there's nobody to eat with you. You don't want to eat most of the time when you're by yourself.

And there ain't nothing to do around here. 'Bout all we can do is sleep. It's about like somebody is dead around here.

And there ain't nowhere to go down here. You go anywhere down here, you're soon's to get arrested and you ain't doing nothing. They always keeping up with the colored people, won't let them have any fun or anything. Put 'em in jail. You be with anybody in a car, well, if he done had a drink of beer, he get arrested. And they say he drunk and he don't be drunk. And so there you go. Stop you on the road, if you haven't been drinking, if they think you been to a beer place or been to Crenshaw to get

enough problems. And me, I have enough. Nobody to do nothing for me, nobody to help me, nobody here to talk to, nobody to say nothing to since Aunt Rosa died, and when the wrong somebody come, I don't say nothing.

Sometimes you want somebody to talk

some beer or been to Como to the whiskey store or have been up to Nesbit to get any beer. If they think you done been up there, they sitting and waiting on you when you come down. They won't put in jail if you ain't got nothing in there but, see, they just going to stop you. And a lot of times, peoples ain't doing nothing, they hate to be stoppeded by the law, you know. And make them feel guilty when they ain't done nothing.

They hadn't never in Senatobia in their life wanted the colored to have no legal rights with them, no kind of nothing. 'Cause if they catch me with a half pint of whiskey at my house now, they'll fine me. And every house of a white person you go to in Senatobia, you'll find a bottle in there, nothing but gin and stuff. But you better not find it at no colored person's.

And downtown, the colored don't go in these places, these restaurants. And it's 1969. That cafe on Main Street, you go up a little alley and you go into the back, and white eats up in the front. Look like a little closet, you know, like a long, little old room back there and two little old tables in there. And you go in there and order your stuff out from under this little window.

And that truck stop on the highway, they've got a room in the back. You can sit down and eat but you still have to get it through a little hole. And sometimes you be in there three hours before they bring it there. Just a table or two in there and that's all. And most of the time when you go in there to eat, the table is full up with cups and saucers and plates. We ain't never had no clean place to eat.

And I tell you, I just quit working Monday. I sure want to tell you this. Quit working Monday and said I was staying home to sit down and rest. I worked for three months and it looked like I had worked three years. For fifteen dollars a week. I worked every day from 7:30—I go at 7:30 and get off at 5:30. Sometime it be six o'clock. And when I would get home, I would be too tired to do anything. I wasn't getting but fifteen dollars a week—fifteen dollars a week!

I was doing in the house for a man and his wife and two children. A little baby and a girl six years old. Well, after I got the television from 'em, I would pay five dollars out of that for it, you see, a week. That'd leave me ten dollars. That's what I would get. I would make up every bed; I would keep the children clean; I iron every day just about. I cook dinner, clean up the dinner dishes, mop the kitchen, run the vacuum cleaner, run the buffer, get down on my knees and shine the floor. And that just last week. Had to put the polish on the floor with my hand, and I don't know nobody done that in a long time. And so I just quit.

He said I wasn't going to have nothing to do but tend to the children. His children was the importantest thing. And when I got there, when I got in, you see, then he started putting it all, everthing. Everything was on me. And I didn't know I had to cook; he didn't tell me that. I didn't know I was going to have to iron every day; he didn't say that. I know maybe that I was going to iron sometimes, but you know, you just iron, iron, iron, iron.

I worked with their children and other folks's childrens too. Every day *all* day. There's three other little old children used to come over there every day and stay over there and worry me all day long. That's why I be so nervous. That's how come I'm like I is now. I'd be so nervous, I wouldn't know what to do. When I come home, I couldn't sleep at night. For I could hear them children go, "Jessie." Just calling me. "Jessie, Jessie,

Jessie, Jessie." And I told them I wasn't going to quit and so I didn't quit *then*. I stayed at home that Monday and rested. So the next time I just quit. 'Cause I wasn't getting nothing. Nare a week I got paid, wasn't hardly get enough to buy rolls, wasn't enough to buy me a pair of shoes or nothing.

I knowed it wasn't right. I knowed it wasn't right, because after I been so good and done all the rest of the things and every week I'd go, they add something more onto what I was doing, out of all I was doing. They add something else different I had to do. Okay! Every Monday morning there'd be something different. I'd get there Monday morning, he leave and go somewhere. Okay. He said, "Jessie, feed the hogs." The hog pen is 'way out yonder. Okay, I walk that far in grass this tall and I already had told him, standing right at the gate when he hired me, you know, that I was scared

of snakes and that I didn't like to get in no grass. And he said, "Well, you won't have to get in no grass. You just tend to the children." See, and now he sended me to the hog pen, then he sended me to the pasture to turn the cow out.

Well, I'll tell you why I think he treat me like that. There's *one* of my opinions I know. It's because they think we don't know no better. That's one of 'em. I think they think we don't know no better and they think we should just do that, whatever they want us to do. For that little a money. I don't mind doing nothing that they would want me to do if I was getting paid good. See, when I go to work, I wants to work, but I don't want to work for nothing. That's all the difference.

I think of my ideas like this. If we all could get some things that we needed . . . we *need* these things—that's why I think everybody so evil. Because we need it so

95

bad and we been needing it so long. A good house to live in. Good food to eat. Good clothes to wear. If we just had that, I think that it wouldn't be all of the fighting and evil [rioting] going on in the world that's going on now. But we can't get no help. We hadn't had no help. But if we just would get help, just enough to feel a little better. And any human being need a good place to live and some good food and some clothes to wear. That's the way I think about it. And if they would get them things, I think that it would be better. Wouldn't be no more fighting and nothing they could be evil about because everybody would have something that they really need real bad. And them three things what we really need bad.

Because, see, we done worked and worked and some of 'em, the older peoples, just done worked till they just gone down. All right, they get their welfare checks. Okay. That don't be enough for them to live out of hardly, but still they makes it off of that. Everything that they give us, it be just enough just to do whatever it call for.

So some of these kids now, maybe twenty or twenty-one, they hadn't been to no school. I mean their father and mother didn't have no money to send them to high school and get an education. See, they just went to school and got out of school with no education. Well, they can't get a job. And that's what make them so evil, see. They wants to work and want to have something and can't work. 'Cause they didn't get no education. And I think that's the biggest problem. I think it is. That make all the evil go on.

I've thought about leaving Mississippi. Yes, I want to go. But I ain't got nothing to go with. I haven't got transportation money and I have to have something

96

till I can get me a job. Any day I could leave here, I leave. Minnesota, where my auntie lives, is about the place I would want to go. I think about it all the time, of going there. She want me to come over there and stay, you know. I don't have to live with them; just so I'm there.

I was going to get a job up in Minnesota when I visited there, and the man where I was going to get a job at, the place wasn't going to hire till August or September, and that was some switchboard operators. And you make two-hundred dollars a week. And just look what I had if I stayed up there—two-hundred dollars a week! And from last August to this August I would've had it pretty good, wouldn't I? 'Stead of getting fifteen dollars a week down here.

I had that in my mind. I was going go get me a job and get me an apartment and live up there with my auntie, where she was and the childrens all. She wanted me to live there where they were. So the man told me, "Well, you can get a job. Ain't no need worrying about getting no job. You can get good jobs in this city. Some womens make more than the mens do up here." And so, well, I went up there that day and saw where they wanted them girls, where they was going to hire twenty-some girls last August or the first of September. And so I said I was coming down here and go back. And when I got down here, ain't never got the money to get away from here to go back on. 'Cause you got to have or starve. I didn't want to go up there and be on nobody. I always like to be so I can do things for myself. I don't want to go up there and my auntie have to do this and that for me and stay with her.

Now, if I had childrens—I don't have any kids—but if I had some, see, I could go up there to Minnesota and wouldn't have to worry 'bout the children. 'Cause

they do for the children. Just like new-born babies, they give 'em a shawl. I don't care what color he is, give 'em a

shawl. And the girl, when the baby's born, she just go up there to that big store, to the office up there, and bring back a whole big basket full of brand-new baby clothes. Sure do. My auntie's little old daughter, after her baby were born, she went up there and got hers. The other little girl, when her baby was born, she went up there and got hers a shawl. And so I thought that was real wonderful. But you ain't going get nothing down here. Ain't going get no shawl. The baby might be put in jail or something.

I just say I'll stay here till I get me enough to leave off of. And when I do, good-bye Mississippi. I don't want to see you no more. Ain't nothing here—nowhere to go and nothing to do. And they won't let you work. They make you stay at their house and they work and get all the big money, the big job, big factories. Make the colored peoples babysit. Nothing wrong with that, if they want to do it. But I don't want to do it. *I* don't want to babysit. I want to work at the factory, too. And make me some money where I can live comfortable a little bit. And not all the way, just part of the way would feel better than like I am now.

6/ *Ada Mae Anderson*

"Ada Mae's the fishingest woman I ever knowed," Rosa Lee says. "She fish near about every day except Sunday. Better watch out for her down there in the bottom—she liable to be tromping through there toting a big old catfish, heading back home. Ain't never seen nobody who can catch 'em like Ada Mae. She might be splashing along through that there creek. Ain't no telling where she might be coming from. Fish everywhere."

Scores of zinnias at least four feet high fill the garden in Ada Mae's front yard, which boasts one of the few lawns in the area, and Ada Mae keeps it neatly trimmed. Kudzu vine shrouds her house and forms a leafy screen around the front porch.

An old shotgun leans beside a chair in a corner of the porch. Many black people's houses in Mississippi have at least one shotgun, sometimes two or three, for hunting and protection.

Ada Mae, whom friends affectionately call "Cook," keeps a patch of corn, butterbeans, tomatoes, and okra, and raises chickens, and she usually has something warm on the stove.

She quit playing music several years ago, but once blew the harp with gusto and sang in a voice "like a man's."

I'm fifty-two. I was born in Panola County. We all stayed around in the same community. My father was making music and farming a little—George Hemphill, Sid Hemphill's brother.

My father, he was a good man. He was real quiet. And he was a good musician all right, played guitar. He wasn't rowdy at all. And he didn't believe in no whole lots of roughness. He wasn't no Christian, but he acted better than

I've seed some Christians acts. I never heard him cuss in my life. And him and my mother stayed together fifty-two years and I never seed him hit her in his life. They never passed one lick. I think he was a real sweet man.

Now, my mother—she living with us now, she eighty-two—she pretty rough on us. Well, she believe in the right things and wanted us to learn to have manners for old peoples, treat everybody right. I wouldn't say she was rough. I would say that in them days, but I don't say she was rough now. Because I'm glad she raised me like that. I know how to treat people and I appreciate the way she did raise me.

But I thought in them days she was rough. You had to do what she'd tell you to do or she'd get you. You wouldn't want her to get you. She would whup you, you know. I'm telling you, she was rough on us. I got scars on me now, I can show you where she whupped me. I'd say she beat us, that's what I'd tell her, say in them days. I'll tell you, in my younger days, I thought my mother was the meanest woman I ever met. I used to tell her, said, "Mama, I declare you the meanest woman I ever seed in my life." Well, that woman have whupped me so, I'm telling the honest truth. Had to grease me to get my clothes off. You'd have to do what that old gray-headed woman tell you to do. If you didn't, you'd of wished you hada.

But I see the way people raise children now, she did the right thing. Biggest portion of the children now, they raise their parents. You can't find no good-raised children much. Now, in some ways, I'm rough on my children. You have to teach a child the best way you know how. And if the next person, they teach 'em this, teach 'em that, and the way they looks at these old TV's and one thing and another, they already bad enough, they'll soon get out of hand.

But I ain't as rough as my mother was. That don't be no more. Not like my mama raised me. See, my mama talked to me, but look like she would whup more than she would talk. Well, now I try to talk more. Talking do the best. It's just like me. If you tell me, say, "Ada Mae, I want you to do such and such a thing, if you can," I'll try to do it. But now if you tell me, say, "I mean for you to do such and such a thing, and you *better* do it," well, that's going put the devil in me and I ain't going try to do *nothing*. And so I figured I'd give a kid a chance like I would want to have.

The first memories I had . . . I don't know how old my grandfather was when he died, but I can remember when he died. And I know I was a little bitty little something then. But I can remember when he died. And I remember him

'cause when they had him swaddled—they swaddled him and put him in a casket—they didn't put him in no undertaker shop then. They had him in a room and he had real curly hair. And he was bright, kind of looked like a white man. And I went in there—they had him laying on the cooling board and they told me he was dead. And I told 'em, I said, "My granddaddy ain't dead." They said, "Yes, he is." And I went in there and he had some matches in his mouth to keep him pulled. And I went in there and saw those and took those matches out of his mouth and put 'em in my mouth. I can remember that. I sure can remember that.

Now, my worst memories is when my brother got killed. I was eighteen. I don't know what year it was. He was grown. Named Joe Lee. That's a long time ago. Another boy shot him. His name A. W. They claim that this boy had been beating a girl and my brother stopped him from beating this girl. And so A. W. told him that he would see him later. So A. W. came over here one morning and me and him went to the cornfield to get some roasting ears. And I told him, I said, "You go get the rutabaga, I'll go get some watermelon." So he went down there to get the rutabaga and stayed so long that I called him and asked him, "You want some watermelon?" He said, "No."

So we went on to the house and he kept straight on up to the white people's house. And my brother was up there. And some of 'em say A. W. said, "Well, you call yourself bad over yonder to the picnic the other night. I'm going see is you bad now." And he shot him.

Well, A. W. come right by my door. And I said, "Run, A. W." See, the white man had been saying that he come over there with a pistol again, he was going take it. And I thought A. W. and the white man had got into it. I was telling him to run.

And just as he got by the house real good, my youngest brother, he run in. He said, "Where the gun? Where the gun?"

I said, "What you want with the gun?"

He say, "A. W. done shot Joe Lee."

And I said, "I wished I had've knowed it." The gun was sitting right at the door. If I had've knowed, I'd of sure shot him. He was close to me here. I was telling him to run, thought that the white man was after him and he had done shot my brother! And got away. That hurt me worse than anything. I think about that a heap of times now. But I reckon it's better I didn't know that he had shot my brother 'cause I the one been sitting in jail right now.

Now, the best memories I had—the

most fun I had back then—was when I went around with Uncle Sid and the girls to pick up the picnics and things. Now after I looked like I going give music up, it don't never bother me. But in them days I wasn't satisfied lessen I was around where the music was or was trying to do some of it. I played the guitar and blowed the harp and beat the kettle. And played the bass violin. In them days, you run a bow across the strings and then you work your fingers and ooh-doo-do-do.

I'd leave home and stay with them for long times at a time. I just went around with them. See, they wouldn't hardly farm. They was just making music, and I just traveled around with them and make music with 'em. They went different places in the Delta and just go around to people's houses and play at night.

Just like Sid would be at a picnic or

something. Now, he would play for a supper, call it a breakdown. But he wouldn't play no longer than twelve o'clock. Then us girls would play. We'd get the band then and just keep the music until day. Yeah. He'd just take his fiddle and things and sit back. And say, "Y'all girls can take it." And we carried on.

I danced a little bit at the picnics, too. I, you know, just a person to have fun. I don't call myself a dancer. I just have fun. They had picnics all through the week and every Saturday mighty near. They had picnics—had one here today, one over yonder tomorrow, and one over yonder. Just go out there and barbecue hogs and things, go to eat and knocking sticks and kicking wheat, and just having a wonderful time.

I used to sing in a gospel band, too. We had a band and . . . what made us break up, our president, he drank. And when we would get to singing, he would just break in and sing with us, and we wouldn't want him to sing with us. And we just got disgusted and quit. Gospel band. There five girls. We would sing jubilee songs. Sing at different churches. About in '30, somewhere along in there.

I was singing blues, too, then. I like to hear blues and to sing 'em. But, now, they don't take no effect on me like a church song take. I can get more out of a church song than I can a blues. I have been a Christian sort of person all my days. Before I even got twelve years old, before I even got old enough to go to the mourning bench and get religion, I always been on the Lord's side. But still, I would do these things, but I wouldn't mean 'em. I'd do that sometime to have fun. Just like I'd jump out here now and dance and a little bit of something or other like that. And it don't bother me.

See, I don't think it is evil to sing blues. You know, God will forgive you for anything you do, mostly. You know, that's possible. Like, things that you don't do *too* bad, you can easily get forgiven for it. It just like this—if you got anything *in* you and want to do it and don't do it, it's a sin to not do it. If you do it a heap of times, it'll leave you. And that's the way I was about the blues. If it get with me and stay with me, sometimes if I didn't sing 'em in two or three days, they just stay with me. Then when I'd sing, they'd pass on off.

See, people's be's in a different mood. Just kind of like a feeling. Now, there's some peoples that wants to hear church songs and then again they want to hear the blues. It's the feeling. That's the biggest portion of it. It's the way it make you feel.

Now, I quit playing music . . . Well, I just left here and went North—Gary, Indiana—and I just stopped 'cause after

I got up there, there wasn't no visiting and wasn't much fun, no more'n going to the beer tavern, things like that, and so I just put the guitar and harp down. Up there, I worked in cafes a little and housecleaned a little.

Well, there was right smart of things I didn't like about Mississippi, but I could do something about some of 'em and I just went on and did it. 'Cause I could leave here and I didn't have to work here and I just went on to the North. Here you would make a crop and you had to take half of it to pay your debt, and if you didn't pay your debt you would still be behind, and in those days you have an old debt, you'd have to pick it up the next year. And so you didn't get what you're supposed to get. I just 'cided I could put it down. I did put it down.

I liked it fine up North. But I didn't like it and I never will like I do my home.

I don't believe there's nowhere they could carry me that I'd like better than I do Mississippi. I guess because I was born and raised here. And though up North they treat peoples good and nice and everything, but still I like my home.

I come back here in '44 . . . I think it was in '44, and farmed six years. Frank, he went to the Army, and they sent him down South, and I come back here 'cause every time he take a furlough, he could come home. And that was closer for me to be down here. And that's the reason I come back. After he got out the Army, well, my father got in bad health and I just stayed on here with him. And after he passed, my mother, she was old and she got in bad health. And I stayed on here with her, because I knowed she couldn't stand that climate up there in the North. So I just stayed on here.

Besides, I like the country better 'cause I don't have to buy no license to

fish here. I have to buy a license to fish in the city. I like here better than Gary, Indiana. I ain't sitting on no water, and I ain't much scared of a bomb out here.

You take when we stayed up there, my husband driving a bomb every morning when he go to work. And that got me scared. And when he cut out and went to the Army, I cut out and come to Mississippi.

I would go back North, but it look like it's kind of opening up back here. It's much better than it used to be when I left here before. We got a little better opportunity than we been had. And then look like we get a little more every year than we been. Got more privileges. And then it's a lot of places that I couldn't used to go, I can go now. You take . . . I used to have to go around to the back, I can go in the front now. And then I can go to their churches if I want to go. I can go to their homes, sit down and talk with 'em like I want.

Look more like, you know, we done got together now more than we did in them days. I's been knowing all the time we all is peoples, but we was separated. So I feel more better now 'cause I and real nice little white girls, women and girls, and I believe if I need accommodation, I could go to them and ask them and they give it to me. And then I could go to 'em and enjoy 'em and I believe they enjoy me. Ain't like it used to be. I enjoy Mississippi more now than I ever enjoyed.

I'll tell you. I been taught about the races ever since I got up pretty good size. I always had good white friends when I was little, and we would go together just like these children do one another 'round here. And I was always taught that they was white. See, we could get out and play with the childrens. And, you know, call 'em by their name until they get up good size, then we had to Miss 'em or Mister 'em. My mother and them always taught us that. "Now you can play but . . ." Always a certain distance that you

110

can go. "Now they white. You can't associate with 'em." Now they taught us that.

But now we always had white friends. I mean, like I'd get ready to play, white people's children would say, "Ada Mae, where you going today to play?" I say, "Well, I'm going to the Mound. I'm going to a picnic," or something. And they said, "Mama, I want to go with Ada Mae."

Well, sometimes, they would let her go. Go to my party, riding mules and horses then. Put 'em up behind and carry 'em on with me. I remember I carried Lurleen Dougherty to the Mound to a picnic with me. She cried to go with me and her father and mother let her go with me. Sure did.

Well, I thought what my mother told me was like she said. I thought it was wrong to do the things she said not do. I didn't know why. But I knew this. I knew our race was dark. Some of 'em was bright, but they still was a color. And the white people was white. I know there was a difference somewhere, but I didn't know where. They was white. And we was black.

Treat 'em nice, just like, you know, if they ask us to do anything—"Come over here and do such and such a thing and I'll pay you or give you something"— well, we'd do that. If they tell us to do anything, we 'sposed to, you know, say "Yes'm," "No'm," "Yes, ma'am," and "No, sir." They taught us that. And we knowed not to sass 'em, curse 'em, or hit 'em, or anything like that. Because we was taught, if you would do anything like that, well, the mob—that's what they called it then—the mob, they would kill us, you know. Just like if me and you get to fighting, and I hit you or something or other like that, well, you go get somebody to come in and maybe kill me.

111

Or either kill all my people. Well, it have been done, and that's what they teach me. And I would stay with them, be with 'em, but I stayed in my place.

Now, I teach my children just like my parents teach me. But in these days, it's different. The mobbing part, it ain't like that now. Just like now if I had a boy large enough to court, and we found out that he liked a white girl, well, the biggest thing to do is to send 'em away good. Make the boy go or the girl go. They used to would kill 'em, break their neck, and one thing and another like that if they was courting one another. I remember my second cousin—least they said she got killed on that account. They broke in the house on her, kilt her. And they said that was the cause of it—courting a white man. But it ain't like that now.

Well, I'll tell you about me. I have lived in the North. But here's one part I didn't like. Associating with the whites and all things like that, I don't want any. Now, I got plenty white friends. I have et with 'em, have drove with 'em, sat in their lap, have slept with 'em. But I ain't one for that there mixing stuff; I don't care for that. I ain't never liked that.

Here what I want: If I go out there and go to work, Mr. George come out there and go to work, too. And if I work long as you work, pay me off, too. And if I go and speak, I said such and such a thing, and you said, "No, that ain't true," well, my word ain't no good. Because you white. I want to have my rights in that way. Not for this other, I don't care for that. I don't think about that. Some people got that wrong. I done got too old to think about that anyway.

Now, here what I'm talking 'bout. I don't want to mate with 'em. I 'sociate with 'em, why sure. We can lay down there together and sleep together, but

112

what I'm talking 'bout the chance of crossing my side up with yours. That's what I'm talking 'bout. I love white people. Them that, you know, treat me like I'm human. But you know what I mean.

Now what would I look like if part of my children be white and part of 'em be black and they all mine. I wouldn't like that. I wouldn't like it if some one side and some the other side. Now, I teach my children that if they, you know, would do a thing like that, they couldn't stay here and do it. But what they decide to do after they get grown, that's left up with them. I was talking 'bout Ada Mae. What they decide to do, that's their life. They got to live it, just like I live mine.

Now, I was always taught to say "Yes, ma'am" and "No, sir." But when I went up North, they told me 'fore I got there, said, "Now, don't say 'Yes'm' and 'No'm' to 'em. Say 'Yeah' and 'No.'" Well, quite naturally, it sounded, you know,

kind of outlawed to me in a way because I hadn't been used to saying it. And it kind of embarrassed me.

So when I first went up North, we had a grocer. We had an account. So I went on to the store to get some groceries and the man, he was waiting on me.

He said, "What else do you want, Mrs. Anderson?" And I told him. And he said, "You say you want something else?" I said, "Yessir."

He stopped just as nice. He said, "Mrs. Anderson . . ." I still said, "Yessir?" He said, "Don't say that." He said, "We don't get that up here. We say 'Yeah' and 'No' to everybody."

Well, you know, I felt funny because I had been always saying "Yessir" and "No, sir."

So he told me, he said, "Now, we is just as one." Said, "Now you say 'Yeah' and 'No' to me, and I'll say 'Yes, ma'am' and 'No, ma'am' to you."

113

I said, "Why is that?" That's what I said.

He said, "That's just the way we are." Said, "Don't say that." Said, "I know where you from. You from Mississippi." Said, "We don't do that up here." Now he *told* me that. Sure did.

Now, here's part of the problem, the way I see it. See, you try to do something and you hear some of these other Negroes around here. "Ada Mae trying to do so-and-so. She think she something. She this, that, and the other, she think she white, and, oh, she try to be more than anybody else." That's the way the peoples is. They don't pull together enough. They always trying to down you if they see you trying to pull up, trying to down you some kind of way.

And so I just figure that if Negroes could get together, all of us could just be like sisters and brothers. That's the way for us to be, but it isn't going to be like that. "If so-and-so going buy more than me, I want a nickel of it if I can get it. If I can't get it, I'm going steal it or take it." That's the way we is.

Now the white race of peoples is better than we is in a way. Now, if they see somebody trying to pull, they going get behind 'em and pull 'em on a little bit. If our race be pulling up—"You know so-and-so yonder, he think he white. He think he this, he think he that."

I'll tell you why they say that. Because they don't want to be nothing but a drag and they ain't going be nothing, and they want you to be it. If you try to be somebody, they going try to pull you down where they is 'cause if they ain't going up, they don't want you to go up. If you hold yourself up, you're too much. Well, if you get out, drink like they do, get drunk, cuss, and raise sin, one thing and the other, you be buddies then.

I been married once before I married

Frank. He named Albert Gater. I was fourteen when I met him; when I was sixteen, we were married. I don't know why we got married, 'cause I sure didn't want to get married. He just out-talked me, I reckon. He just tried to show me the place where he could take care of a wife, you know. And he wanted a wife. It was a good while before I'd give him an answer. But I finally went on and married. It worked out pretty good for about six years. Then it got on the rough side.

He was jealous, for one thing. And I say I was kind of mean, or something or other, and I would jump on him and fight him. And so we just got to the place that I would try to hurt him real bad. And so I just left to keep from hurting him. See, I going whup him so he couldn't do nothing to me. He jealous, see.

He jealous . . . 'cause there's some peo-ple just jealous, I guess. I don't know why. I don't know whether it love or not, but they want to fight you sometimes. Well, look now, here's what I can't understand. You love me, you said. But still you'll kill me. And what you going love me and kill me for? If you kill me, you won't see me to love me. Now, why you want to kill me? I just can't understand. Now, you know when they put you in the ground, you ain't seed no more. Well now, you go and love me and then get me out the way. Just like if you have a piece of furniture. Now I love it. You ain't going try to tear it up and you ain't going hurt it. 'Cause you love it. Why's it different with women? And men. They want to kill one another. So how do you explain that? I don't think that's love. I don't think they know what love is.

After we broke it up, I went around to picnics and things. Dated once in a while. And then I fooled around and got married again. To Frank Anderson.

I met him at a church. He was a Sunday school teacher. And he asked me to let him go home with me. And the funniest thing about it, he lookeded just like a preacher; I thought he was a preacher. I thought the preacher was meddling, you know.

And he said, "Can I take you home?" I said, "Nope." He said, "Why?" And I said, "One thing—you didn't bring me."

And I said, "If you had've wanted to bring me to the church and come to the home and got me, then I'd of come to the church with you." And he said, "Well, could I come and get you and bring you to the church?"

I said, "Maybe sometime." I said, "I'll let you know." I said to myself after he left, "Now, what that old preacher keep on meddling at me for?" I found out later he wasn't no preacher. We laughs about that sometimes now. I thought he was a preacher meddling.

How come our marriage has lasted so long? It's the way you handle marriage. And then sometimes you're not got the right person. You got to cooperate together. You got to be digreeable. And you can't marry just to spite somebody or "I can get him," or "I'm going get him," or something like that. You be made up in your own mind. And if you say you love, act like you love. Now, if I love you, I ain't going misuse you. Well now, if I'm going treat you any kind of way, even if you do love me, you going on to somebody else. There's people out there will treat you nice if I treat you wrong. Well, you can love those people out there. The nicer you be and the more you *try* to be nice, well, that'll make it hold you together longer.

But if you go to spatting and going to saying, "Well, you going out, doing so-and-so, and you staying in their own doors doing so-and-so," well, you look to not to get along. First thing you know,

116

one will get hot, and they going do something to the other'n or the other'n do something to the other'n, seem like. That cause a separation then. That red piece of flannel can ruin you, you know. That's your tongue. You got to hold your tongue. Sometime you can't speak when you want to.

Now, I got two children, ain't my own. That girl there, I'm not her mother. She was gave to me when she was going on two weeks old. And I raised her until now. And I don't believe that I could think no more of a child than I do her if it was my own. I don't see but one thing —I just didn't birth her.

Jimmie Lee Sawyer, that was her mother's name. Well, she was single, and she was just, you know, going through the world. And then she was having children and staying there with her mother and her mother didn't like it. And so she would give them away. She gived away another one. And so she gave me this one

and I take her and been doing all I can for her ever since.

And the little boy, that's my husband's kid. He was going on six years old when I got him. See, after I found out that it was his'n . . . that's what I'll show you 'bout love. I love my husband. And if I loveded him, I couldn't despise his child. I love his child. And I asked his mother to give him to me, and she gave him to me, and I don't think no less of him than I would a child of my own. He's going on thirteen. She going on fourteen.

Now, I hope they'll have a good education and have a long life and treat people right and be a good church Christian. And, you know, try to have something, and don't just throw away everything they get onto. And I do hope that they'll be treated in a way better than we was because they got a better chance now than we did. They got a better chance to go to better schools. They got a better chance of learning more. They can hear

117

more on the radios, and they can see more on TV. And they know more 'bout news. When I was a kid, I didn't know nothing 'bout news, no more'n what the peoples tell me. And now they can hear it for theyself. They got a better chance than I had.

Since I quit farming, I ain't been doing anything but just taking care of my mother. I just got tired of farming and we wasn't getting nothing out of it. But my husband, he's disables to work on the farm. He can't work on the farm. They don't allow him to work at all. He got a disabled check. And they don't allow you to work when you get a disabled check.

Now I just fish every day. Fish three times a day if I can. I leave house 'fore sun-up, come back around ten, eleven o'clock, see how my folk getting along, and then I go right back. And it get hot on me later on in the afternoon, I go

back. I catch catfish; catch breams, crappies, bass, and channel cats. If I don't catch nothing for a few days, I feel worser than I felt in the front about going. That don't bother me really though —'cause they don't bite. I know they got

118

to bite because they going get hungry. Had a lot of 'em tell me, say: "You go to fishing every day and the fishes ain't biting?" I say, "I don't know when they going bite, but I want to be there when they get ready."

Now my home is my main satisfaction. My family, my home. And when I got them pleased and got everything going along smooth, I'm satisfied. I got more interest in my home and my peoples than I is anything. I don't have nothing for the world. Course I go out and have fun sometime, but my life is at home.

Well, as far as the future goes, I'm like the old song, I ain't thinking about dying. And I'm hoping I'll live a long time. And I think it's a right smart of happiness for me.

Ada Mae: Who in the Hemphill family will keep music goin'? Well, I don't know, but . . .

Jessie Mae: Well, my Aunt Sidney in Minneapolis, she got some girls; she got four girls we can teach. She got a girl that's training to pick guitar, and I been in Minnesota, and I teached her how to pick guitar. She wanted me to teach her how to pick. So I learned her how to play a few blues and church songs. All the rest of 'em are small, Aunt Sidney's grandchildren—she got four of those—and I teached those how to dance. I'm going still teach them younger children how to play music and how to dance. I want the Hemphill family to keep on going.

Ada Mae: Well, the way I feel about it, and the way it been all the time, there's a lot of Hemphills you didn't learn nothing. It was in them already, I guess. And I believe long as there be a Hemphill, they going do something— dance or preach or make music or something or other like that.

119

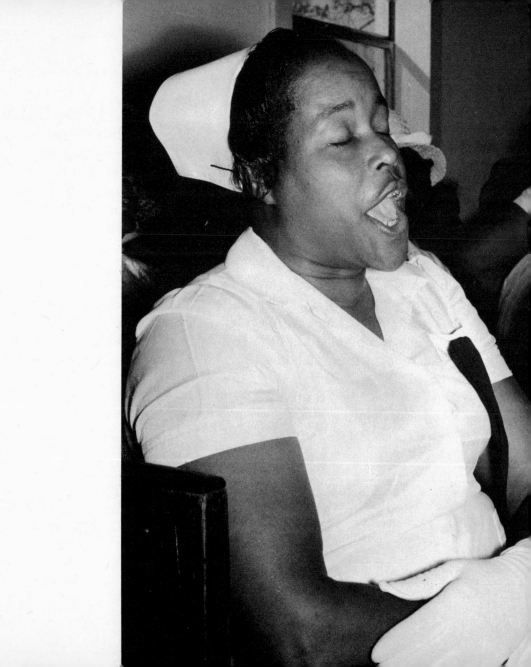

7/ *Let the Spirit Come Down*

New Salem Baptist Church is about three miles down dusty gravel roads through the cotton fields off Highway 51 near Senatobia. Members of the congregation are proud that it is a new, white, block building instead of a more typical crumbling wooden one. A cross tops its small resolute steeple.

The Sunday service usually starts around two o'clock, shortly after Reverend M. B. Chaney arrives from his morning service in Tunica. But pickups begin to pull up to the yard well beforehand. Other members come on foot. Presently, the men gather around the preacher's car to discuss Abe Callicott's leaving his wife for Chicago and how a dog over at Hawkins' store went mad. Inside, the women stand around talking about the sad death in the Turner family and a certain church member who has not been present for eight consecutive Sundays.

At the appropriate time, the men walk gravely into the church and gradually take their places in the straight-backed pews on the left, while the women and children sit in the middle and to the right. The head deacon reads from a large, worn Bible and the treasurer scans the ledger at a table facing the congregation. Dime store religious prints dignify the walls and an old upright

piano stands in one corner.

The service is emotional—sometimes mournful, sometimes tense and feverish —and there is a strange, beautiful kind of unity among the congregation. When one is moved to pray, he prays out loud. The others hum in harmony and interject their feelings when the spirit urges.

The ceremony throbs throughout with song and rhythm. The preacher half sings, half shouts the sermon, while the congregation encourages him with ejaculations of "Hallelujah," "Praise the Lord," and "Oh, yes." They want to capture the feeling of the spirit more than the sense of the words.

122

An elderly man kneels on the floor and pleads wailfully in prayer:

Lord, have mercy this evening.
Give us more love in our hearts.
Oh, Lord.
We're living in a war-torn world.
Let the Spirit come.
Open up our understanding,
And let your wisdom come down.

A voice from the center of the room rises in the first three notes of a song, and all the others join in.

Gaining strength from a hope of happiness in death, they sing out:

When you hear my horn blowing,
don't worry about me.
Yes, when you hear my horn blow-
ing, don't worry about me.
I'm fixed up right now, yeah, yeah,
I'm on my way home.

One thing I know that I been born
again.

I made preparations one Friday
'cause, Lord, I didn't know when.
When my Lord call me, it'll be my
time to go.
I'm fixed up right now, yeah, yeah,
I'm on my way home.

When you hear my horn blowing,
don't worry about me.
When you hear my horn blowing,
don't worry about me.
I'm just another soldier, yes, yes,
I'm on my way home.

Sleep on, my mother, don't you
worry about me.
Yes, sleep on, my mother, don't you
worry about me.
Your child fixed up right now, yes,
yes, I'm on my way home.

Finding comfort in the knowledge that Jesus was also persecuted, their voices rise:

When they crucified my Lord,

Oh, when they crucified my Lord,
When they crucified my blessed
Savior,
Oh, Lord, He never said a mumbling
word.
Only He just bowed, oh Lord, His
head and died.

Oh, when they whipped him up the
hill,
Yes, when they whipped Him up the
hill,
Oh, when they whipped my blessed
Savior,
Oh, Lord, He never said a mumbling
word.
Only He just bowed, oh, Lord, His
head and died.

Oh, when they nailed Him to the
cross,
Yes, when they nailed Him to the
cross,
When they nailed my blessed Savior,

He never said a mumbling word.
Only He just bowed, oh, Lord, His
head and died.

Oh, when the blood come streaming
down,
Yes, when the blood come streaming
down,
When the blood come streaming
down,
Oh Lord, He never said a mumbling
word.
Only He just bowed, oh, Lord, His
head and died.

When the moment appears right, Reverend Chaney steps slowly up to the pulpit. "I'm tired. I been up all night preaching and I been preaching all the morning. So I'm just going tell you a parable and maybe I'll get into preaching."

"Okay, preacher, go ahead," the members of the congregation answer.

124

"This professor, he couldn't get no job and he saw an ad in the paper. He went and talked to the executive and the man told the professor that the teacher always gets beat up. So school started Monday morning and children was coming down the alleys to school. First thing he did was sing him a song. Then after he sung, he read the scripture. After he got through reading, he sung him another hymn. Then he got down on his knees and asked the Lord to help him teach.

"Then he wrote the rules on the blackboard: No stealing in school. No lying in school. Anybody who breaks these rules gets a hundred whacks on his naked back. Little Johnny stole a lunch.

"The teacher, he said, 'Little Johnny, did you steal that lunch? Can't you read?'"

" 'Yessuh.'

" 'Pull your shirt down then.'

" 'Professor, let me by. Don't whip me, let me by.'

"His hands were pausing, eyes sunk in head. 'Reason I stole that lunch, I'm hungry, got no mother or father, don't have no home, slept under the bridge.'

" 'Johnny, that's a sad story, but pull down your shirt.' "

Preacher Chaney begins to chant.

"This kid in the back, he say, 'Professor, stay your hand.' "

"I hear you," the congregation joins in.

" 'I got a mother,' he say. 'I had a good breakfast. Let me take his place!' "

"Hallelujah," the members sing.

Preacher Chaney paces back and forth and raises his arms.

"Lord didn't tell me to pray, He told me to preach," he yells, his voice raspy, grating.

"Okay, preach then. Preach."

"I was getting raggedy."

"Sure 'nuf!"

"Shoes getting holes in them."

"Go on, go on!"

"Food running out."

"That's right!"

"But I kept a-preaching."

"Oh, Lord!"

"We ain't 'shamed of our God anywhere."

"No, we ain't."

"We'll call Him anywhere."

"Sure will!"

Feet begin to tap, keeping up a steady beat to the rhythm of Reverend Chaney's words.

"God made this here world."

"Oh, Lord, lift me up!"

"He made me and you and our enemies."

"Lord, have mercy."

"You gotta be good to your enemies."

"No, no, can't be!"

"Yes, you gotta be good to 'em!"

"That's right."

"It nice to have the devil around. It makes you pray more."

"Come on up there."

Some in the congregation sob; one, seized by the spirit, screams.

The Reverend spreads his arms. Sweat runs down his face. He cries out:

"Oh, yes, Adam and Eve was living in the Paradise."

"Lord have mercy."

"She ate the bad apple and offered a bite to her husband."

"Tell the truth, brother!"

"Soon as Adam ate the apple, his personality changed . . ."

A good sermon will go on for hours. It may be suppertime when the members of New Salem Church file out of the small white building to face the coming week.

8/ *Robert Johnson*

July is cotton chopping time in the Delta. Although new weed killers and fertilizers have cut down on the need for their services, some whole families still get up at daybreak and, carrying hoes, walk to the fields where they will remain until late morning. They return in early afternoon and stay until the oppressive sun goes down. Theirs is the most tedious of jobs: raising the hoe and slamming it against the ground, breaking up the dirt and thinning out the weeds, hour after hour. A gallon jar of water is kept in the shade of the nearest tree, and one of the small children occasionally lays down his hoe to get it and haul it out to the field. For this drudgery, each usually gets no more than fifty cents an hour, but if a mother and her five children are working, they then can buy more food than they will be able to at any other time of the year.

Few motorists turn off Highway 61 about three miles south of Cleveland toward the small Delta settlement of Skene. There almost every resident, from the plantation owner to the hand laborer, looks to the cotton plant for his living. The modern brick home of the owner of the huge Circle H plantation sprawls on a landscaped rise overlooking the shacks and tiny frame houses of his

white agents and black field hands that are set here and there in the ocean of cotton.

It is here in the fields that Robert Johnson can be found slaving in the scorching July sun with his hoe. If an outsider drops by, he might stop his labor for a minute to exchange a few words while he mops the sweat from his face.

"Yeah, I play church songs . . . They say it's going up to 104 today . . . I'll be out here for the day. You come back tonight, I might play you a couple pieces . . ."

A cloud of dust down the road heads

his way and shortly the "manager" is climbing down from his pickup. "How you coming along down here, Robert?" Robert's hoe is again in use.

As a man gets old, he's got to start preparing to meet the Lord. Many older men who have been singing and playing blues all their lives resolve to sing only gospel or "church songs." Blues is an evil music, according to beliefs in the Delta. As the elders of one congregation warned an aging blues singer: "You better quit singing them blues. You ain't too old for the devil to get you."

But Robert doesn't need anyone's warnings; he was warned by God, he says, some seventeen years ago, and he has played nothing but church songs since. For Robert, to start singing blues again would be to shake hands with the devil.

Robert still plays in the old Mississippi bottleneck style. The neck is broken

off of a fifth whiskey bottle and heated to smooth down the jagged edges. The guitar player then puts the bottleneck on his little finger or, like Robert, places a pocket knife between two fingers, and as he picks the guitar, slides it over the strings, making them cry and whine the tune.

All of Robert's children, from his four-year-old son to his pretty teen-age daughters, are gospel singers, the older ones quite accomplished. On sultry

nights they get together on their front porch to practice with their father, and the message of the Lord flows out over the cotton fields.

I was born in 1916, the fifth day of December. I was born Crowley, Louisiana, on a farm. That's where I was born. I was three years old, we came to the Delta. My mama came here; my father came, too. My grandmother and all of her children. There was a gang of 'em. Moved out here on Number 8. Out east of Cleveland.

My mother, she was a maid. Worked at white people's house. She didn't like it so well, but she had to go along with it. Wasn't getting nothing for her work. She wasn't working for no salary in them times. Working for whatever they gave her. And times they give her maybe a couple of dollars or some meat or some meal or flour, something like that. After I was big enough to understand some things, she just would tell us what she went through with. She told me how she worked, how she worked for flour and meal and a little piece of meat, sometimes a hog bone.

But she didn't take it hard. She said it was a brighter day ahead. She said if you trust in the Lord, one day it will be better. What she said, in life, she didn't worry too much about it, but you know she had to worry some.

She was a church worker. And she was a good cook, she loved to cook, houseclean. That was what she loved to do. It was a belief she had in life. She didn't go about. She wasn't a lady to go about. She be around home all the time. See, back then, I imagine girls wasn't allowed to go out like they is now.

I got eight girls. See, they go to school, but they wants to go out. But I don't care 'bout them going out. I tell 'em when they get grown, get on on, they can go where they want to. I let 'em go out sometime, but I don't just let 'em go out to go around and in these cars and like that. They can get hurt in cars, and boys drinking and going out. And then some of 'em out, they think they'll have some money and they rob you.

Now, my father, oh, he was a man . . . He loved public work. He farmed till '27.

Then quit farming. He went North. To Chicago. I was round about eleven or twelve years old. My mother didn't want to go to Chicago. He went and stayed, and he come back, but still she didn't go. He went back; he didn't come back no more. She just didn't want to go to Chicago. I think she liked the farm more better. But he could make a better living up there. He worked in a steel mill.

When he was here, he was a good father. In vouching for his family. Raised hogs, chickens, had a pretty good ordinary living. Back there nobody make no lot of money. You raise what you eat back in those times.

Back there, see, people making crops, but ain't nobody fooling with making no crops now. Nobody making crops, sharecrops, now. See, people working on the farm by the day. And lot of people got tired of the farm. Trying to find something else to do.

Day labor is better. Oh, no, not no sharecrop, 'cause sometime you make all that cotton and then didn't make nothing. Now, make you twenty-five, thirty bales, the man tell you, say, "You did good." Right in the heart of wintertime. You put all your labor out there and worked right up in the wintertimes, he settles with you and then tell you, "I think you did good." You ain't cleared nothing to carry yourself through the winter, buy you no clothes or nothing. Now the owner, sometime he get all of it. Some of 'em, you know, settle with you pretty good, some will let you make something.

I think I made only one crop when I didn't get anything. I was successful when I was farming. Made some money mighty near every year.

Now, today, I do day labor on this place. Me and four other fellows chop cotton where it need it, the others drive tractors and things. Work ten hours a day except during harvest time, then I work overtime.

We got agents that supervise us. Got around about five agents. What they like? Well, they try to get out of their place sometimes, but you just have to go on on. Some of 'em be off in a pickup and see us stopped or taking a rest period and here he come. See what you doing. Just tell him, "I know I have to work for a living, I'm out here to work." Just talk. When he say something to me, I say, "Well, I'll work but I ain't going run." His main problem—the agent's—well, what he's doing, 'sposed to be looking out for hisself, too. Some of 'em just glad of their job. The boss man, what we're working for, he's just paying them a salary, too.

Now the owner of this place, Johnny Howarth, well, he's a pretty nice man, sure is. He's a pretty nice fellow. He told me he didn't style me with some of the rest of 'em. You know, you have labor on a place, different types of people, drink, throw everything he gets his hand on, always wanting to borrow money, and always into something. Big place like this, you have all types of people on it. See, I never ask him for nothing unless'n I has to have it, which is very unusual.

I don't get but a dollar and thirty cents for working. Anything I do, that's what I get.

Do I think I ought to get paid more? Oh, yes. Never asked him for it. He wouldn't give it to me. Well, he have their own view. See, people in this part of the country, they ain't never paid nothing for work. And they think paying a dollar and something an hour, that's a lot of money. See, they ain't never paid nothing for work. Now, what I think . . . I don't think but one thing—we ain't getting enough. At least high as the cost of living is, I know we ain't getting enough. I just thanks the Lord for what we does get. Because we used to not get that.

Now see, this man owns about eight plantations through here. And what I was telling you this afternoon, that's just too much land for one man to own. While there are a bunch who can't get enough to get buried under. What I was talking about: you take, the first man the Lord formed from the dust of earth. Come out of the earth. And we know, sure as you be born in this world, sure you going die. You know that. But men got all this land and the Lord call you out of this world and then you ain't got nowhere to bury your body. You got one of these men sitting out here with thousands and thousands of acres of land, and you got to pay, I'll say, about twenty-five dollars for a grave. And those men sitting over there on thousands and thousands . . . Won't give you just a grave to bury a body. And that body is going back to mother dust. And they won't give you a spot of grave if the Lord call you. Every man on earth is entitled to six foot of this earth. *Every* man that born in the world.

And he entitled to more than that. But a poor man, he always have been kept down. He ain't had no show. Long as you got to look up to the other man, you see, he keep you down and keep you looking up to him where he can give you what he want. Long's he keep you down, you obligated to him. And that's why our race is so far back.

But things are getting better now. These times today was to come from the foundation. The world is based upon one thing; the world is changing; time bring about change. See, if the time had've stayed like it was back in them times when I was coming up, wouldn't nothing

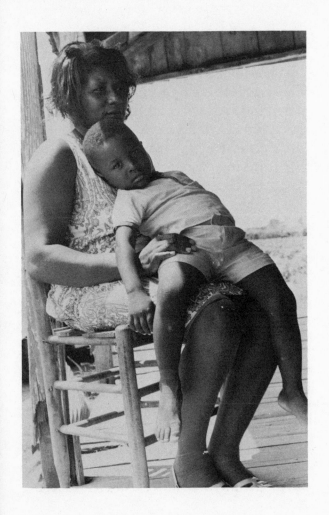

developed. Time moved us out of that, moved people out of that. And our people yet still looking for better in the future now. That's what people looking for now, looking for better. It's better now than it was back in those days. Much better. Lord done brought us a long ways. And nobody bring us but our God. But we had to go through that. We had to go through that time.

But now we got better schools to go to. And we have . . . Well, I say all the way around it's better for the colored people than it's ever been in the history of life. Oh yeah, I think it will still get better. The world ain't going back. The Lord don't carry nothing back. People carry things back, not the Lord.

See, the Lord, He *help* us to make it better, but if we want to look for better, we have to do better ourselves. That's something we have to do. See, we put everything on the Lord, but that's some-

139

thing we got to do. If we want the world to get better, it ain't going get no better less'n we get better. If it get better, we is the ones to make it better. Everybody 'pending on the Lord to make it better, but we is the one—here—to make it better.

I was a kid when I learned about the races. I was taught by my parents. In those days, they would teach the children to stay in they place. Obey. In those days, just like if some of 'em do you wrong, you just go on and don't say nothing, just forget it. Don't argue, don't fight, don't do nothing.

Well, I thought that was a good policy. Old people back then, they believe in the Lord. They believed in the Lord would bring them out from under bondage. And they know the Lord wouldn't bring 'em out fighting back. They meant you had to be meek. Meek mean humble. Sometime you have to take things.

I still believe that way. I know now. There are things you have to take. See, the man that own a lot, he don't know he got a date. I don't care what he own, he got a date. He ain't thinking about that. He thinking 'cause he got a lot, he always be like that. But he got a date. Then when he get too high, sometime the Lord have a way of bringing you down.

Now, my own children, I tell them . . . See, I couldn't teach my children really proper in their days like I come. 'Cause it's much different. What I tell 'em, I teach my children this: Learn how to treat people. We all are human beings. It's your main problem in this world; learn how to treat people. If you know how to treat people, you can make it anywhere. That's your first step in life.

How should they treat a white person if he don't treat them right? Well, I don't care how much education a person have, he have a date. And he doesn't know when the Lord's going call on him. When you are carried before the Lord, don't be no polices, no judges, no presidents, no priests. Any man got to give an account on his own. You're living for another home. See, some folks on this earth, that's their heaven, right here. That's how come they're cruel and mischievous, lot of folks. Want to take over. But the Lord, He one man you got to go by.

So I teach my children . . . I don't mean stand up and just let 'em push 'em, beat 'em up. But you got to learn to take things. Like a person say, "You're a nigger." That don't mean nothing. Anybody can be a nigger. A nigger just is a slander word. Anybody, it don't make no difference what nationality and color you is, anybody can be a nigger. We have a lot of Negroes and we have some niggers. A nigger will do anything, but a Negro won't. Anybody can be a nigger. It's just a slanderous word, that's all.

See, I used to play for white people—parties. Well, you have some nice white people; in all races it's good folks. But, in all races there's some mischievous people. That's the way it is in all nations. You take a lot of white people, they got good hearts just like some colored peoples. Colored is just as mischievous, don't make no difference what nationality you is. The way I see it—and that's the way the Lord sees it—that you heard mischievous people in the Bible, how mischievous they was, that's in all races.

I was around eight years old when I learned to play guitar. My uncle learnt me. All four of my mama's brothers could play. He sat down and take my fingers and place 'em on the notes. And place my fingers on the strings. And let me flail it. And he'd take it hisself and I'd watch him, how he'd work his

141

strings. And I just caught the sound. And I come just playing myself. Wasn't over eight years old.

When I was in my teens, I was playing for white and colored. They were doing the two-step. Along in them times, boogie woogie wasn't out. Two-step, waltzes, biggest they'd do. I'd be playing 'bout "I'll be coming 'round the mountain when she comes" and "Ain't going rain no more." Oh, they had a big time. In they days, it just like it is nowadays; they had as much pleasure with that they days as folks have now.

Course in them days, folks wasn't mean as they is now. At parties. They wasn't as mischievous. I remember some rough times, but, see, people in those days, they could talk to people. If something like that start or somebody get into it or something, they'd go out there and talk to him and shame him out of it. But now, you can't do that. They get mad and they won't let you talk to 'em. They want to do something to you.

Blues hadn't reached us. I imagine it was in other places, in other states, but when it got here, we taked hold. I started playing blues when boogie woogie begin to come out. It was a change. Change in the dancing, change in the music. I liked it. I could play "Drifting Boogie" and I could play "Pine Top Boogie," and I had a piece, blues I'd play 'bout "I'm broke and I'm hungry." I'd play 'bout *I'm broke and I'm hungry, ragged and I'm dirty too. If I clean up, pretty mama, can I go home with you?*" I had another blues I'd play, "*She's little and she low, she right down on the ground. She's a tailor-made woman, she ain't no hand-me-down.*" See, folks was going for that.

Sing blues for myself or others? Well, when you're took with a piece you're singing, you're singing primarily for yourself. Course some of the blues took

142

with the musicians like it did other people. Made him feel good. It made me feel, oh, uplift. See, that's what make you play. You get high up and play. And you get on a piece that will suit yourself. And that's when you go to work, then, for other people. And, oh, a heap of time, they's clapping their hands, patting their feet, hollering 'bout "play till the cows come home."

Far as money, when I played for white people, I wasn't on a salary. They just passed the hat around in the house. And all what money put in that hat, that go to the musicians. But when I was playing just out for a juke or something, a ball, when I was hired, I was playing for a salary. I'd make all according to how long I'd play. I'd play sometime all night. If I got paid up to twelve o'clock, I'd make around ten dollars. Ten dollars a lot of money in them days.

Blues make me popular with ladies? It didn't make me popular with the ladies, you know, in this instance. When you're a musician, you got to know how to meet the public. Course you meet so many ladies out that say anything, that you got to have some brains yourself. You may meet one and she may be staring right at you—you a single man—and you say, "You married?" "Oh, no, I'm not married." Husband may be standing as far from here to over there. I see in my career when I was playing out, just like I was playing for you, I would tell you, "Don't let the ladies get 'round me." When I was playing out these places, they had it fenced in. Roped in. They had some stakes up. Couldn't anybody get to the musicians. 'Cause see, that was dangerous. But I had some in my band, he get to drinking, he go talking baby stuff and might say "baby" to the wrong man's old lady. That cause somebody to get hurt. You see, that's why I had them fenced in.

I played music until 1927 when I joined the church. That was the first time I quit making music. Saved in 1927 on a Wednesday. A revival. When I was first converted, I didn't believe it. I went back home. I asked the Lord to show me was I converted. I choose me a spot of clouds, and I told the Lord, "If I've been converted, let that spot of clouds vanish." When I said that, the clouds just did like that, just like my hand. I testified in life for that more than once. The clouds didn't just vanish even, they just moved away like that. I asked Him to do it. The Lord will do things for you if you actually mean it. Just like something you wants to know, He know you means that just from your heart, He come quickly, sure will.

Now, when I was singing blues again, I got out of the church. I don't believe in being in the church and doing that. I got

out. When first joined, quit playing. I went back to playing in '30. I got out 'cause I knew I couldn't serve two masters.

See, I was in the church at a young age. I hadn't been out in the world to have no pleasure. And I let the devil persuade me to go back to that. It was in my mind, see, that made me do that, go back to making music. But I was out of the church.

No, I didn't join too young. But, you take a young person, he liable to join a church and he liable to get back out there and get to dancing, doing different things he have did. But up the road he'll come back. He can't stay there.

Now, what made me come back, I done got older, and I seen so much happening, seen people dying in all different forms, and people just walking falling dead, and I got to thinking about myself. I played blues clean up until 'bout '52. I just couldn't go no further in it. Heap of times I'd be out playing and something would just speak to me in my mind and tell me, say, "What if you die in this shape?" Something just say, "What if something happened to me?" See, lots of things happen to a person playing music. Lots of things happen. Sometime you get hurt off suspicious thoughts. Like the lady-folk want to hear you and they say something to you and a heap of times people gets the wrong impressions.

Now, what I mean 'bout dying in that shape, I know if the Lord called me in that shape, I know my soul would be lost. And that just stayed on my mind. I had to quit. You know that not the way of the Lord, if you're going play blues. You're on an occupation of your own. You just out on your own. Well, the Lord can't get no glory out of you when you play blues. See, the Lord get glory out of you. Such a thing as playing

church songs, that's how He gets glory out of us.

Church songs, see, make you feel uplifted to the Holy Spirit. Sometimes you can get out a church song and you get so happy you can't sing it. You can't utter your words. You just get all shouting. It don't come all the time, just sometime. You start giving the song out, and sometime you get pulled right in here and water just pulging out your eyes.

Oh yeah, evil spirits have you happy too. See, I didn't know what made you feel good back then when I was playing blues. I didn't know like I know now. That evil spirit make you feel happy just like the Holy Spirit. It make you feel good, but still it's an evil spirit. An evil spirit have you in that form, but you ain't on the Lord's side. Singing the blues. And then he can't get no glory out you.

If you don't want Him, He don't want you. That's how come the world's like it is now. Lot of people think today 'cause they getting along good, don't serve the Lord, don't think about doing His work, think he just getting along without serving the Lord. Which he is. But he don't know he got a date. He got a date coming. Then when something happens, when these things come up on him, then he going call upon the Lord. But the Lord won't see him then, you wait too late. When the fear come up on you—when these things come—just like sickness and, you know, we have all different problems in life . . . Sick days come. Something hurt you, the first thing you going say, "Lord." When you mash your finger, you're going say "Lord have mercy" or something like that. But no need of calling on Him, you won't do nothing He say once He gets there.

You may be getting on, be getting anything your heart wishes, you done forgot

146

the Lord then. Because you got a fine automobile, may have a good job making good money, you just figure you ain't got no date. But things can hit you, paralyze your whole body. Then you start calling on Him. But it's too late.

Do I ever lose faith in the Lord? Never! Never! Because He's been too good to me. I can show you what instance. I was working for Mr. Charles McCutchins out here from Indianola. I was driving a tractor and I'd been up the night before. That first mind that come to me told me, don't you go anywhere tonight, you go home and go to bed. And so I had my mind made up; when I quit work, I was going on home and hit the bed.

But instead of me following my first mind, I let this fellow out-talk me to bring him to Boyle that night. He told me if I'd bring him to Boyle, instead of driving the tractor I could go out here on this road and sleep, out in this ditch. He said he'd drive the tractor and let me go out there and sleep if I'd bring him to Boyle that night. So I went to sleep out there. Well, I had about fifty dollars in my pocket. I knowed this fellow was a snitcher and I dig me a hole in the ground and I put this money in the ground and I laid on top of it and went to sleep.

So that evening I came on home and I did my work. Then I taken him out here in Boyle. And so I stayed out there all that night and had to work the next day. Sun-up caught me down there on the road, on my way home. Had to go home and milk cows and then get in my tractor and go to fields. Long about ten o'clock, I fell off that tractor plumb into a ditch. I just had a blackout. And I can't tell you today how I got out from under that ditch. I didn't get a scratch put on me. Nobody take care of me but the Lord.

147

That's right, He was the one. Sure was. I know He been good to me. That was in '49. He was warning me.

Then right before I joined the church again—the second time, in 1953—I got another warning. My uncle, he had been down to Cleveland that morning. He went on back home and got his mower and went to the fields. His wife see the mower stopped out there on the end and she decides to carry him some water out there. And then she seed him laying back from the mower, one of these here mule mowers what cut this hay. He was laying back on the mower. She thought he was just playing with her, so she got up a little bit closer—she called him "baby" —and said, "Aw, baby, quit that." But he was dead.

So when they were getting ready to funeralize him, I was over in the fields. Everybody on Sunday was visiting at my grandmother's home, a lot of kin people and visiting friends. I was over in the fields and I 'cided to go home and get ready to go to the funeral, too. I went on home and I went over to her house. And something about my heart went to beating fast, my breath went to just leaping. And I didn't want to tell my wife. There was some alcohol there on the table and I just take that alcohol and went to sachinating my face with it. And I was just talking to the Lord, just talking to Him. I said, "Lord, you done take my uncle." I said, "You going take me with him?" I said, "Allow me another chance." I got to talking with Him and asking Him to spare me and finally my breath went to coming back to me.

That was a wonder. I didn't belong to the church. He was warning me. And next pastorial day, I went to church. And the pastor got up and he said, "The door of the church is open." The minute he said the door of the church was open,

I left my seat, and been joined up in the church ever since.

Now, I got ten children in all. Three of 'em grown, live in Cleveland up here, Chicago, and Miami, and the others live here. All these girls now, they in school. And sure, they work on the farm, not on this one but over yonder. Pick cucumbers —that's what they're doing now—and chopping cotton. All except that little boy and that other little girl. Five of 'em chops cotton. The youngest one that chops, she Vera; she ten. Have to do something to make a living. Picking cucumbers, twenty cents a basket, and chopping cotton, five dollars a day.

I hope they finish school, get them learning. I didn't have the opportunity. I didn't get the opportunity of going to school. I stopped school and went to plowing. I went to school on piece-time. I go on rainy days, and when it was dry

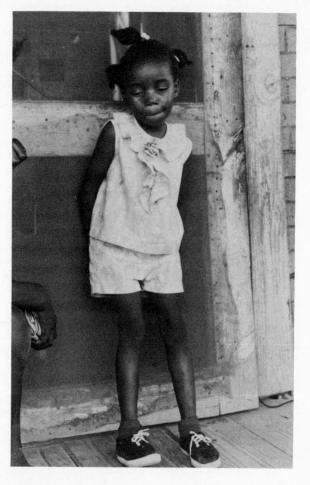

enough to work in the fields, I'd go to work.

And I'm hoping if they get learning, I'm hoping they can get 'em a good, decent job so they won't have to be out doing field work. See, some change made now. Get 'em a job at a hospital, a nurse, or something like that. Any kind of job 'scusing on a farm. I mean, they ain't lazy, they'll work. I mean they don't turn down field work, but in their days they have opportunity.

One thing I would do different if I could live over again? Well, if I had've knowed then like I would have knowed now, I'd started out and got me a home. That would have been my first think. Because in a time like this, what we're going through now, every man need him some place to stay. Need him a home. These are tenant houses, you just stay in 'em when you're working for him.

That's the next step I have in view

now. Try to seek to get me a home. And, well, if a person got a pretty good credit reference, he can get him a home. I guess these other folks around here never trying to seek to get nary'n. I know I got a good credit reference. I think I'm going get me a little place in Cleveland, but I ain't never made my mind up. See, me and my wife talked it over. I don't know, I believe I'd rather buy me a lot. Not just buy one of them houses like they sell 'em, put 'em up and sell 'em. See, they got a lot of houses on these plantations now they sellin' 'em, and I could move one of 'em. Build it in Cleveland, get me a job in one of them filling stations or something.

9/ *William Diamond*

William "Do-Boy" Diamond lives on his "boss man's" farm outside Canton, Mississippi, just north of Jackson. Canton is large enough to have the courthouse shaded by magnolia trees and the square lined with hardware, dime, and drug stores. Popular music pours softly from loudspeakers at each corner, but a block away it is drowned out by the soul music and rock-and-roll blaring from jukeboxes in the section of cafes, poolrooms and barbershops where "Do-Boy" spends his Saturdays.

"Do-Boy" is one of the more fortunate few who have jobs operating tractors and other farm machinery. In back of his house is a mammoth barn which houses the equipment. The expansive cotton fields begin at the edge of his grassless front yard.

Besides working on the farm, he is also comanager, with a white man, of his boss's cotton gin. "Second week in September and we still ain't ginned no cotton. Most every year we start ginning near about the middle of August. Seventy-five or eighty bales a day—that'd be a good day's run. But the cotton just ain't been coming in. Had a late spring and a cold August. Ought to be starting up soon."

"Do-Boy," who no longer plays regularly, wrote or "studied" many of his songs, which usually boast of women he has had. On the occasional Saturday afternoon when someone hands him a guitar, friends still gather around and join his singing with raucous laughter on favorite verses such as:

Best woman quit you, don't you weep and moan
Get another high yellow, boys, and you can carry that same thing on.

I'm fifty-three. Born in Mississippi, in Madison County. 'Bout as far from here down to Cameron's store. Had four brothers and eight sisters in my family.

My father, he never do nothing but farm all the time. He first started out half and half and then he started out to rent. Was working on the halfers. You know, half the crop belongs to the next man. But Papa just said he's giving away too much of it, and then he just

went to work and bought him some mules and quit, you know, and went to renting. And he rented plumb until he quit farming.

I was about twelve when I first started helping him to farm. That's when they farming with mules. Wasn't tractors, they was mules. I went straight to plowing. He started me out young. He'd lower the handles down for me, you know.

I liked it when I first started, plumb until I learned it and then when I learned it, I hated it. Yessir, when I learned it, I hated it. Got tired of it. I'd tell him I'm tired and he'd tell me I wasn't tired, go ahead. I wouldn't do nothing but go ahead 'cause I know if I stopped, he'd of whupped me. We'd work ten hours every day.

My father, he was a kind of a man what didn't hardly ever stay at home much. He'd be gone the biggest of the

154

time. He drunk a whole lot. And he'd be gone. And when he come off from work sometime, we wouldn't see him no more'n two or three days. He'd be gone off somewhere. Wherever they had whiskey, that's where he'd be. Now, I didn't have no think about it. I was small. I wished he was around there more but he wasn't, so we just leaned at the mama then.

He said he was going leave. He was tired of farming and he went to town. Up here in Canton. He didn't never come back no more. Finally, him and my mama, they just separated. He stayed there and I stayed on with my mother. He worked for the city.

Me and my mother farmed on. She worked in the fields some. She got old and then after that she got old, she quit. She worked in the field about twelve years. She chopped and picked cotton.

Mama, she was just a up-to-date lady, all I could tell. She was a good mother. Feed me a lot, whup me if I be bad. She couldn't be beat. She was good and friendly and good to everybody. All the biggest majority of the leading class of white people here in Mississippi knowed my mama. And liked her just like I don't know what. I mean rich white folk. Everyone just knowed her.

Now I was real bad. I was meddlesome and bad. One time I had a little old dog I likeded. His name Mane, just a little old red dog. And a neighbor stayed up there not far from us, he caught my dog in a steel trap and kilt him. And he had a gang of turkeys. And I waited till all of them went on the field. And I run to them turkeys and caught the old gobbler and the hen and picked them just as clean as your face and turned 'em loose. They's live. And went on home. Picked them just as clean as you was fixing to dress 'em and turn 'em loose. Big old

155

white turkeys, just walking along.

My papa didn't whup me about that. 'Cause he told that man . . . him and papa got into it about it. And my papa told him, he pay me for that dog, he'd pay him ten dollars apiece for them turkeys. But if he didn't pay him for the dog, he wasn't going pay him a damn nickel, not for nary'n turkey. They had to kill both of them turkeys when they come out of the field.

Now the person I 'member most when I was a child, she name Oda Bell Barnes. She used to grab me when Mama and them getting ready to whup me and I'd outrun 'em and make it to her. She wouldn't let 'em whup me and keep me there all night till the next day. And the next day sometime she take me back home. She was just a friend lady. And I was so bad, just look like she taken a liking to me. She live right there in Canton now. I goes to see her all the time. She'd keep 'em from whupping me and she seed I likeded peanut candy and she'd send to the store all the time and get me a block of peanut candy. She'd talk to me about being so bad and she'd call me her boy, you know. Mama would always pay attention to her.

What I likeded to do most back then was breaking bull calves and ride 'em. We'd go out in the pasture and catch 'em and rope 'em and put two together and make us a wagon. And hook them scoundrels to it. And they'd pull it, just like a pair of mules. They would've weighed maybe around 250 pounds apiece. See, there'd be six or seven of us. We'd take a crosscut saw and get an old great big tree and saw some round blocks off it. And that was to make us wagon wheels out of. And bore some holes through it and get some sticks and run through it. And take it and tie us a tongue in it. And then we'd hook them

oxens to it. And then we'd get up on that and ride. Had a yoke and put it

'cross the necks. Just all over the pasture and all up and down the roads.

I reckon I was about twenty-five when I started playing guitar, wasn't I, Sally? I used to just go around to where the old boys was—boys was playing guitars and one thing and another—and I used to go around to dances. Oh, they was good dances. Them womens be flat-foot shaking it, and them people cut up with them guitars. And I said if ever I got to be, you know, my own man, I was going learn how to play a guitar. See, my papa, he wouldn't let me out. I wanted to go to 'em, but he wouldn't let me. Said I didn't have no business at 'em. If I went anywhere, I had to be back before dark. Now, when I got up in age, I'd go to them dances and I'd stay till they over with. Listening to them guitars. Then I picked it up myself.

Why do I sing blues? I don't know, I

157

guess it's just a habit. I just don't know how it come to be a habit, but just got in my mind when I was singing 'em and I just lit out to singing 'em. Wasn't nothing else for me do. That's the onliest thing that pacified me. Make me feel uplifted and such a thing as that. Don't be feeling drowsy and dead, drowsified.

Just go along studying about one thing and then another'n. Sometime I get to studying 'bout some girl friend, lady friend on my mind. I can't get chance to see her, then I go to drinking and singing the blues.

Is blues always sad? No, blues not sad at all. No, sir. They're lively. With me. Now, I don't know about nobody else. But they're lively with me.

Now, in my way of thinking, blues is mostly for the other people listening, not for myself. Look like they enjoys it better. Make it up for myself. Then later I sing it for other peoples. I be just going along, studying about something and just get to thinking about it. And then I just go on and make up a song and then when I get it kind of like I want it, then I sing it for everybody can hear it.

I guess I sing blues about women all the time 'cause I like 'em. I didn't get married the first time till I was about thirty-one or thirty-two. Had to do a lot of picking. Didn't want to be too fast. I believe women liked me then as much as I liked them. And, ooh, that was fine with me. I believe women liked me on account of that guitar, some part of it. My singing was some part of it. And I don't know the rest of it.

If I seed some woman I liked at a party I was playing at, I wouldn't do nothing till I could ease around and get a chance to whisper something to her. Ask her is she married, what her boyfriend name, or something like that. That's what I get around to asking—

is they married and where they live at. They tell me they see me at such and such a time. The first time I met Sally [his wife], I had my guitar. I believe I got more womens than men what didn't play guitars. The lady-folks then, you couldn't find many of 'em don't like music. But some of 'em say they don't like a man play guitar 'cause there's too many womens pulling for him. See, you may find one or two like that and the rest of the womens wrap a man up playing guitar. They can't hardly play for 'em shouting and going on over him.

Now I married Sally 'bout twenty-one years ago, ain't it, Sally?

"Be twenty-four."

"Twenty-four years ago."

Sally: I was already there at a dance. I didn't know him. I just seed him when I was down there. I heard 'em making such a maouration, I went to the door to see what it was. I heard talk of him, but I had never seed him, didn't know him. "Well, Lord, you want to hear some music, you let 'Do-Boy' Diamond come." When he walked up there, I heard, "Do-Boy Diamond." I broke to the door and they was toting him. I said, "Well, that man must can do something. Them men's toting him in.

"Do-Boy": I've been quit playing about seven or eight years. I just quit. Just quit all them guitars and give 'em to the children. Just to get rid of 'em. Sometime I still go 'round to a dance and the dance going good and, you know, get two or three drinks of whiskey, and those old guitars be sounding so good and then I sit down there and play a couple of pieces myself. Kind of keep in practice a little bit, you know.

Just got tired and just quit. People worried me so for dancing, man, I get to the place I couldn't sleep none. I couldn't rest; and the weekend and Friday night, it be someone wanting to hear me a dozen times. Just play a little while, and then when I get that, he keep me all night, all tomorrow, that Saturday, all that Sunday, and up until that Monday if I would just stay. My fingers would be so sore I couldn't even ball them up.

Now, on Saturdays, I just like to, you know, frolic around. Just go to town. Go in them cafes and one thing and another. That's the favorite one, what they call "Green Moon Cafe." Go somewhere and buy me 'bout a half a case of beer. And just drink it till I go to feeling good. I go get it sometime and bring it here, or either it's a cafe right over the hill down there, then that bar be open or either I go down there. They got a jukebox in there and they dances and plays the jukebox.

Sure, I've heard work songs. You could hear people then, 'way back in them fields and things, working. Hear 'em late in the evenings for miles, almost two or three miles, singing. See, they be in different fields. There'd just be a big plantation full of people and every man would have his own field. And late in the evening, go to get before sundown, quitting time, then you hear 'em go to singing. Ooh, it sound good. Great Scots above! They be plowing and talking to the old mules. And they'd be singing. Just be singing to themselves. But everybody could hear 'em.

I got four children living with me now. My dead sister's and my niece's children. Two of 'em my dead sister's children and them two little boys in there my niece's children. She lives here. Bill, that's my baby sister's kid. He was nine days old when his mother died. We raised him. He thirteen.

I got this hope for them—after they

started to working and know to do and they get on a job somewhere, I hope they pay them wages, you know, just like they pay the white people. Especially if they doing the same kind of work. Now, that's one thing I hope they do. If they pay white people two and three dollars an hour, pay them the same thing if they doing the same work.

Now, I ain't got but three kids of my own. I got three daughters. One in Ohio and two in Chicago. When they left here, one was about twenty-four, twenty-five years old. She just left, she was grown, she just left with her mother. One about seventeen and the other about nineteen when they left. Both left with their mother. That's my first wife. That was in about from '45 to '46, something like that. They told me they was going with their mama.

What happened between me and their mama, I don't know. I was just . . . The

blame was in me then. I was just, you know, with them guitars and too many women was pulling at me, that's the truth. That was just what 'twas. I couldn't settle down. Too many womens. And I just wild then, you see. Didn't know which I wanted. That's what happened with that.

I ain't no member of the church. I just haven't never joined. I ain't made it up in my mind to go to church 'cause if I do go to church, I want to live for the church. I just don't want to go join the church, you know, then get out and do the same old things that I been doing and knowing I'm doing wrong. When I join the church, I want to join for the church.

There's some work I like better now than plowing. That's with these tractors and things. See, these tractors and

161

things, you be riding all the time. You see, they got a fast way now with the farms. Mighty near everything now what you use on a farm in making cotton and corn, you generally got machines to do that with. Well, you ride them. You ain't never walking.

Yeah, they got machines to pick cotton with now. Some of 'em have a little cotton picked by the womens picking it. But the biggest of 'em got machines to pick it with. Machines put lot of people out of work. But didn't put me out. 'Cause I work with this here man here. This his place. And I been living with him now about twelve years. And I picks cotton sometime with his machine and then I run that gin down there.

I got the job at the gin . . . I was a little ole boy and it was a white fellow taking after me. He was an old northern man. I's goes to see him regular now. He's down here off of west of Madison.

Now, his home in Chicago, on the shore of Lake Michigan. That's where he was born from.

I was hanging around the gin down there. They was ginning cotton then with steam. I wasn't nothing but a little old boy. And he taken a like to me for some cause and he picked me up, you know, and spanked me. I wasn't but about eleven years old. He picked me up and spanked me, you know, and go around. But yet and still, I wouldn't never get out of his way.

So, finally, he made a tall stool—he'd rake that cotton . . . See, cotton comes in now by its own power, but you'd have to rake that cotton in them boxes then with a stick. Well, I wasn't tall enough to stand up there to rake it in. So he made me a stool, and stood me up on that stool. And started me to work there. And paying me a dollar a day. Wooh, man, I was glad of it, I didn't know what to do. Just couldn't enjoy it enough. He just partly raised me. And ever since then I been right down there at that gin.

Then the man running it, he retired. See, he stayed there fifty-two years. When he retired, he let it over for me to run. That's when I 'come manager running it. I just worked myself up. You see, just worked myself up where I knowed everything about it.

I felt good then. They told me that they was going put me there for the head general. I could hire me a helper or pick anybody I choose to help me back there at the stand. And anybody that I wanted, I could go ahead on and get 'em and it be satisfaction with them.

I get paid pretty well, but I think I should get more than forty dollars a week. It ain't none of these in Mississippi— these farmers—going do you justice. Not out on some farm. It's just ridiculous, that's all it is. But yet and still,

you have to try to do it to live.

They's a lot of trouble getting jobs,

163

the colored people do. The first they going hire is a bunch of white ones. And
then if there be a space every once in a
while, they'll whip a colored person in
there. Plenty of people done tried to
get jobs and they couldn't get 'em. That
girl there, Emma Jean—that my niece
there—she been running for the last
six or eight months, trying to find a
job. Everywhere they go, they tell . . .
What they tell you, Emma Jean?

Emma Jean: They tell me they wasn't
hiring anybody, not any colored ladies.
Don't have any openings. Said wouldn't
hire no colored ladies.

"Do-Boy": Yessir, she been trying for
the last six or seven months. And she
ain't got hired yet. And if she ever do
get hired, she get hired somewhere
where she be getting the least pay it is
in rotation. Getting lower pay than anyone else.

Now the only thing you can do about
this stuff is just put some good people
up yonder in Washington and a good
President and put some good people, you
know, in the Senator up there, what's
going help the poor people just like they
do the white ones. That's the onliest way
you going stop it.

I believe the riots, they going help.
Because look like, you know, when you
got a fire started and if you don't keep
it a-going, it will go out. But if you
keep that fire burning, finally it's going
burn on up. And that's the way I believe
'bout these riots and things, is these
people keep a-marching and going on
against these things, I believe it will
help.

I was about seven years old when I
learned about different races of peoples.
My mother and father taught me. They
taught me there was white and there
was colored. They said stay in your place
around white people. Don't sass 'em, you

know. Stay in the place. Don't give 'em no sassy talk if they is talking to you. Oh yes, they taught me.

They just said that we was colored and the other people was white, couldn't go to white places. They said, "No, that's the wrong . . . you can't go to them places. Them white folks' places." They didn't say what the reason, but just said we couldn't go to them places. 'Cause didn't nothing go there but the white folks. It was places when they first started taking us to town, in the cafes and one thing and another. You know, they had them places there for cafes and one thing and another for the white people. We'd be with Mama; she'd have us. And I'd be telling her to go in there to buy me something. Told me no, she couldn't go in there, them was white folks' places.

I told my own children the same things. But, you see now they done gone up the country, I reckon, where the white and the colored, you know, all associates together. They didn't come along like that when us come along. There the white and the colored, the biggest of 'em, associates together some places up there. My daughters used to be, you know, answer everybody, "Yessir, No, sir." But when they come here now, they don't know no "Yessir, No, sir." Just "Yeah" and "No."

Now I don't know whether that's good or bad. I don't know how to figure about that. I just figure that's the way it is up there. Think it should be like that here? Yessir, that's the way I feel like it. If they could do it up there, they could do it here in Mississippi.

The first white people I knowed and likeded when I was real small was this man named ———. He named my brother the morning my brother was born. We was living on his place. And he told my papa to name the boy after him.

He was a farmer. He was a fine white feller. That was 'way back, too. He stayed at us house—we was small children—he have stayed there two and three nights and days. At the house. He be on one of his drinking sprees and wouldn't go home. He'd be drunk and wouldn't want to go and he'd just stay with us. And if he did act like that, he'd have him a couple gallons of whiskey. And he wouldn't go nowhere till he drunk all of that up. And plenty of time, when that get drunk up, he'd send my daddy somewhere to get him another gallon.

He and my daddy drunk together. Yessir! It was just anytime when he got ready. Anytime. Wasn't no special time. His boy would come out there looking for him and he'd be out there. Mama and them tell him that where he was. And he turn around and go on back and tell 'em to take care and if they need anything for him, to go on to town to get it, to come on by the office and he'd give 'em the money and let 'em go get it for him. He was a fine white man, that he was. If you got in jail, you wouldn't stay there no longer than he got the word. He'd come and get you if he had to fight the chief police.

Now, my childrens, the ones here, I done got the notice for I can put 'em in any school 'round here what I want to. I can sign 'em in the white school or either in the colored school. I got 'em still in the colored school. I don't know why I kept 'em in the colored school. I just kept 'em, all. But I think after this go-round, I think I'll sign 'em in the white school. Look like the teachers in the white school take more pains with 'em and look like them learn 'em more than will these colored teachers. These colored teachers sometime don't hardly have a class a day.

I don't know how the younger generation going be. I don't know. I think they going make things better if they keep a-going like they is. Just look like they more for the right things. Like President Kennedy was. Now he was a fine man. Look like he was a better President than any of the others been in there in wanting to help the poor people. That's the reason I liked him. Look like he was just dead for the poor people, and look like he didn't pick his color. He looked like he'd help the poor colored people just as well so as he did the white.

I don't think none of these politicians around here going help the poor. Not around here. It ain't nobody 'round here would help the poor people. All these people down in here, these officers and governors and one thing and another, they ain't for nobody but their race of

people. Now we had a colored man running for Congress here. Charles Evars.

His home right up there in Jackson and when he in the first primary, he ran all over that man. Yessir, he beat him. And on the second when the runoff would come between 'em, they had to guard his house till he could come to the next runoff. He was more for the poor than he was for the rich. I think he'd of help 'em. Made better living for 'em. Paid 'em more on jobs. Paid the colored teachers just as much as they do the white ones. I believe he'd of did that.

He said he going run again. I believe his chances is going be good this time. You see, there's a lot of that that comes in them voting machines. Anytime a man switch and lead a person that far in ahead of votes, and then come back and this man that's almost doubled him again, well, it can't be no more folks vote in the next time. Well, that looks unfair. They'll do it.

Colored people nursing white folks and

cooking for 'em and then not be for them to visit with 'em and sit down and eat with 'em—yeah, I've thought about that. That's ridiculous, ain't it? That's ridiculous, ain't it? Every white lady what's in town has got a colored maid, you know, cooking for 'em, raising their children, nursing for 'em and raising 'em up, something like that. Sure is.

I have thought about that a lots. Thought about: Now, that's something, the way it look like they don't want to coop with the colored people. But don't look like they can get along without 'em, because they going get a colored person to cook for 'em, wash for 'em, they nurse the babies for 'em and they do everything for 'em. And yet and still, that's just as far as they want to go.

Well, see, if the colored person, you know, wanted to do anything to 'em, well, they could get something and put in their food for 'em. And kill 'em. They wouldn't never know it. There'd be too much of it in 'em for the doctor to do 'em any good when he got there.

Now, I've seen white people doing things to colored, beating 'em. I seed that a gang of times. In town there. With walking sticks. Everytime I seed it, they said they was beating him just about nothing. I don't know. Don't happen now. One thing about it, see, the colored people ain't scared of 'em now like they used to be. The colored people used to be just flat-foot scared of the white people. But now they ain't.

Now, I seed one of 'em fighting back at 'em. This man what the colored person was fighting back with, his name Mr. Walter McClelland. Him and a colored person got to fighting right there on the street. And some more white people ganged in there and wanted to help him, you know, to beat that colored person up. And Mr. Walter told 'em wouldn't nobody put their damn hand on him. *He* was a man and *he* was a man. If that man whupped him, it was all right, and if he whupped that man, it was all right. So they knocked at each other, knocked each other down. Mr. Walter knocked that nigger just as flat, and that nigger knocked Mr. Walter just as flat. And they called it off right there. And that's the onliest fair fight I've seed. And wasn't nothing did about it. But the rest of the white people wanted to do something about it, but Mr. Walter told 'em wouldn't *nobody* put a damn scratch on him.

Things is changing some. It's changing, it's changing some. I see the time when I was a kid and now I see it's lots of places that now you can go in since I been grown. And get what you want. And I seed the places you dasn't to stick your head in the door, talking about going in, in these white places. You know,

cafes, and restaurants, and one thing and another.

It's sure changing 'round 'cause you can mighty near go in any of the white places here if you want to and you can get served if you go in there. You know, you want some sandwich or anything and something like that. And, well, you can just step right on up in there and they order it and they'll serve it to you. I haven't never been in there, but I've seed lots more of 'em go in there. I ain't never wanted to.

I haven't never thought about moving North. I got a brother—he be here for Easter—he been trying to get me to go back up the country with him. And I don't know, some of this going on around here, my mind may change any time, I'd light out up North there with him.

I don't know why I stay here. Just staying here, you know, just staying here. That's all, just to be staying here, just by this here being old home. See, I was born just around here in Mississippi and just ain't been nowhere but just staying right around here.

10/ *Robert Diggs*

Robert Diggs lives in Friars Point, an isolated town in the heart of the Delta. It is an archaic town with a sluggish, languid atmosphere. The katydids make more noise than the people. No new building has risen for years in the group of run-down stores which make up the business district. The living rooms in a couple of old, dimly lit houses have been converted into Negro cafes where for forty-seven cents a full meal can be purchased.

As a rule, the houses in the towns of the Delta are not as clean or well kept as the shacks in the country. They sit close together in rows, and automobile parts and discarded cardboard boxes litter the yards.

With modern ideas and aspirations, Robert Diggs's teen-age son looks out of place sitting with his father on the dirty front porch of a shabby house without a bathroom.

Robert and his sister, both blind, traveled throughout the South in their youth playing harmonica together. Because he has rarely been accompanied by guitar, Robert is unusually talented in blending his harmonica and voice into one.

Before relating his life story, Robert hefts the fish his wife and daughter have just caught. Then he takes a can of

173

Prince Albert tobacco from his shirt pocket and rolls a cigarette more skillfully than could most men with perfect vision.

Born on September the first, 1910. Shreveport, Louisiana. Born blind. There was three of us blind—me and my sister and my mama.

We farmed for Mr. C. W. Lang. I imagine, near as possible, imagine somewhere about thirty-five or forty families lived on the place. They paid them for farming. And when they made crops, why, they make a little light settlement down there with 'em. You know, just as usual. He was half-handed with 'em. You know, working on the halfers with C. W. Lang. If you cleared something, you got something. If you didn't clear nothing, didn't have nothing.

My Lord, in them time and day, it went from fifty, thirty-five, and forty cents a day. But when they working a crop with him they would get what you call a coupon to go to these stores, you see. They punched them coupons, you see, for the grocery that they get from that store, and that's the way it go. And then every three or four months, he tell 'em to come up to see him and find some pair of overalls and some shoes and a blue shirt. Well, I want to tell you, to my knowing in a way of speaking, of course, things was very reasonable. They done not quite so good as they did now. But they made it, made a common living by raising gardens and corn and different things. Hogs, stuff like that. Me, I didn't know no better if he give me fifteen cents and I'd leave, and I said it's fair 'cause I wouldn't have knowed no better, you know.

I lived on Mr. Lang's place, oh, about nine or ten years. I picked the cotton. When I got around about five or six years old, you know, like that. Had a pretty hard time. I had to feel for it, you see. Limbs and things be hitting me in the face, but I couldn't of discovered it no better 'cause seems like it couldn't of been no better 'cause I never have seen, you know, to do it. I just went on and done it.

Then we moved to a man's place you call Mr. Charlie Krem and lived there for about three years. We moved to Pine Bluff then. We didn't do nothing. Then we left there. Moved to a place you call Red Leaf, Arkansas. And we didn't do nothing.

Then next time we's kind of getting out for ourself. I used to be picking cotton, the cotton stalk hit me in the eye. I said, Lord, this old man staying in the country so long, ever get so much as fourteen years old, I'm gone. I just knocked about.

The night we moved to Red Leaf, it

was *cold* sleeping that night. We was covered up under the bedclothes in the truck on the way. Borrowed truck. We went on to the house, went to Red Leaf to the house. And my daddy was with us. We all was together then, we all was living. And when we got out, wasn't no fire even in the house. Lot of paper up 'side the wall. And my daddy commenced to tearing the paper down. We told him, said, "Papa, you don't know what you doing." Said, "These people going get after you about tearing that paper down inside that house." He said, "It's cold. Fire ought to've been here. We needs a fire." All right, we stayed there that night.

And it was 'bout six or seven miles, I believe, that distance from there to a place you call Embly. Had a big old commissary store. That's where we take up groceries, there. Papa, he went and got a note from Mr. Stan Reed and Mr.

Kane and give it to us, me—Robert, and Red and Ira. Here we go and went on to the store.

I even went by a man's house, we did, and wanted to warm. And he told all of us, said, "Looka here," said, "Look, y'all know it's cold." Said, "Y'all ought to never left home. You know it's cold." Wouldn't even let us come into his house and warm. Well, we didn't say nothing. I felt mighty bad, that's the truth. It was my own color and you know how I felt.

It was cold. You could see us walking, but we couldn't feel walking. So we went on to the store. And I fell down, I did. One or two times in the snow. It was slippery on me. See, it snowed that night. Well, went on to the store. And we got a package. Well, my sister give Red the receipts to give Mr. Stan Reed. The man fixed up the package and everything, the groceries and everything. Then my

ing." I was 'round fourteen or fifteen. I knowed I couldn't tote nothing 'cause I was too cold. And coming on back we got about a mile from the store, I fell again. And when I fell, it sort of hurt me a little bit, but it didn't hurt me as much as I was cold.

And she had one of those boloney sausage. And she said, "Robert," said, "get up." Said, "Is you hurt bad?"

I told her, "No, I ain't hurt bad. I'm just cold."

So she said, "Get up." Said, "I'll give you a piece of sausage."

I said, "All right, hand it here." She hands me that sausage, and when she give it to me, I got 'way down the road and ate nearly all of it up. Now, I wasn't just doing this plumb out of my head, but I was hungry and cold together. And when them two things go together, it's something.

Got on back home, she told my daddy,

sister turned around and she said, "Robert," she said, "you can't tote noth-

said, "I give Robert a piece of boloney, Papa, and he run on like he et the whole of it."

He said, "Well, don't worry." Said, "Maybe he was hungry."

And Mama told him, said, "No, not maybe. I know they was hungry. They ain't had nothing to eat since yesterday morning."

My daddy said, "Well, be glad for it." That was a rough time.

Now 'bout the furtherest back I can remember, well, that was a bad time too. I reckon I was about five or six, that's the nearest I can remember being that small. One Christmas day my two brothers—I had one named Sam and one named Turner—and they had a cousin named John. And my brother—Turner—got up that morning to walk about some. Him and Sam and John. He give me and my sister Mary—she was a baby then—two little sticks of long candy in our hands. And he kissed her. He said, "I'm going walk about some." Papa told him all right. We was on Mr. Alfred Glassell's place in Louisiana.

That boy was a smart boy. Turner. They all say he was smart, both white and black, and said he wasn't sassy. And so they went on walking. They was going down the side of the creek. There was a road down the side of the creek where they was going. They was walking, laughing and talking.

So there was a guy stayed there called Shag. But his main name was Alex Smith. But all of us called him Shag. He had a little old gray horse about four-some feet. So they walked on down 'side the creek in the road going toward Shag's house. And so Turner went there to the edge of the fence. They had a picket fence around the yard.

"Merry Christmas, Mr. Shag, you and Miss Ludie." He just went up there to

178

the house and told 'em Merry Christmas. Going by, you know.

Ludie said, "Give that boy a piece of cake."

My brother said, "Yassir, I thank you all to the high. But I just don't want me no cake. I don't like cake that much." Well, which he didn't.

Well, Ludie said, "Give that boy a drink of whiskey."

He said, "I don't drink whiskey, Mr. Shag."

Shag, he said, "Uh huh." He said, "You know one thing? Ain't nobody been killed here in seven years. Got to be somebody killed here today if I have to do it, doggonit."

Well, he looked at my brother. My brother told him this. Say, "I hope it don't be me, Mr. Shag."

And Shag, he walked back inside the door and shot my brother one time. And Sam and John tried to hold my brother up. They walk around about, oh, about fifteen, no, about twenty steps, trying to hold him up. So Sam, he came back home. "Oh, Daddy! Shag done killed Turner." Mama, she was sick in the bed. "He said he done killed Turner, Daddy," Mama said. She said, "You hear Sam say Shag done killed Turner." They got an old mule—him, my daddy and my three uncles. And run that guy clean up in Mr. Alfred Glassell's house. Well, you see, they knowed not to go in there. And they begged for him, but they didn't get him. But that guy sent to the penitentiary for ninety-nine years and one dollar a day. He stayed there fifteen years.

A harp the first thing I started to playing. I started to playing when I was 'round six years old. Me and my sister both. I buy one for her and me one. I could get 'em then for fifteen cents. We were small kids and we tried to play up

179

together like that. My sister was about four or five years old. Mary. She couldn't blow too good then. Now when she got into her five or six, she come just making tunes with me.

When we got to be older, didn't do nothing but just went around on different streets and played for different parties, like white or colored. You know, still blowing the harp. We was both of us blowing the harp, see. She learned how to second me. And then I'd play and she'd sing. Don't forget this now, she could second me, too. You think I sound good, I got a sister can rock the blues. Now, you can believe that if you feel like it. Only way I can beat her, just have to blow harder than her. But just for straight noting and playing, I can't do more with her than you can with me. Taught her better than I play myself.

We done that a good many years. I'll tell you, you just imagine us going about through different parts of states. Oh, they pretty well know us. Had to do that by knowing, why that's the way we had to make a living.

I had a guy you call Henry Lee Body. He lives around. He drove for us. He just carried us, you know, and give us water and take us around. Traveled in Arkansas; Mississippi; Louisiana; Alabama; Georgia; Tennessee; Oklahoma; Portland, Oregon; all out there. Everywhere.

I never did take no guitar player. I tell you how I get 'em. I run up on boys in these towns, you know. And I'd get with them boys what had guitars. See, a musician's kind of like a drinker, kind of like a gambler, they going associate with one another.

Jackson, Mississippi, and New Orleans, Louisiana, was the best times I had. I going tell you something. I remember this. I remember one Sunday

180

night. I played for a guy you call Monroe Lewis. He had a midnight club on Rampart Street. And I played for him. And the wonderful time that I had! He had a loudspeaker 'way at the back end of the club. And he hooked it up and had one of them mikes out there on the front, you know. You know, one of them loudspeakers out there on the front. And my God Almighty! Lot of soldiers boys was there that night. Man, listen. I'm going tell you this. I bet you we made around over $150 or $200 in that place. Yeah! Now that's a lively time!

Well now, the reason why that I sing the blues—when I was out in the world depending on that for my living, the biggest of the people'd inquire for 'em, you see. And I'd walk in a place, maybe one fellow would tell me to play him a church song and I'd play that, he'd throw me a quarter. And then around about two or three would ask me to play them the blues and they'd throw me four, five or six dollars. That's right.

Listen, blues and the church songs both run this-a-way—what the Lord intend for you to do, you going do that. Now listen, I didn't have no kind of way to make my living 'cause I was a blind fellow all my days. And the good Lord above bound to had some hands in both of them things, for me to make a living. The Lord gives everybody a way to make a living.

You know blues strike your heart just like church songs do. A man asked me once to play the blues for some church people. All of them went to patting their foot. And so one of 'em asked the preacher, said, "Well, what you patting your foot for?" He said, "I'm patting my foot because all music is good. Strikes everybody sometime." Now a church song will make you feel as good as a reel. 'Cause music ain't but music, and a song

181

ain't but a song.

But the blues, that's what I first started on was the blues. And I made 'em up as they come to me. You can be sitting down sometime, and you can get to studying over where you been or over what you done did, thinking about your people and how you done scatter since

you been some size, don't know where a portion of them at, and that song strikes you. Then after it strikes you, you going study up this-a-way the song that you going try to sing. You going try to sing it away in the time that you was around them. And the first thing jumps in your mind, you wonder will you ever see 'em again. Now, that's one. Well, that'll fall on you. The next thing jumps in your mind, wonder is they dead and gone. Well now, you going sit down then, that's going go mighty hard to you, studying. You going sit down there and you going sing a song that you used to sing around them and then you going add to it. Well now, you going make up a song right from that. If you got any remembrance and can recollect anything, oh, you can just make up a song just like I'm talking now.

Well, my sister and I quit traveling in '46. Got in bad health. See, she been operated on seven times. And then I suffer sometime. I got spinal trouble, stomach trouble, and side. That's the reason we split. Then you see, she married, too, and split from me. But we didn't split 'cause of that, because the way we was going, how we was doing, we wasn't thinking 'bout getting married. What we looking for be money. She got sick and I got in bad health. Sorry, but what's going happen to you's going happen.

Since then, I moped around a little bit by myself, with some different fellows, you know. With "Do-Boy" and "Boot-jack" and different of 'em. Played in white people's houses and colored. And then for little parties and fish fries and all like that. And then—see, I couldn't do much of that. I was lucky enough to get on welfare. First time I ever been on the welfare in my life was in 1938. Wasn't getting but $6 then.

I stopped completely traveling in '47. When I quit, in '47, I lived in Morgan City, Mississippi. I didn't do anything then. Kept blowing harp by myself. And if somebody come want me to hit it, you know, play it with them. After I left Morgan City, I come to Clarksdale. Stayed, laid around the house.

When do I feel the happiest? The happiest thing that I be is when I'm getting them stamps. Course, I be's hurting all the time. But when I go there and don't have no trouble with my stamps, I be happy 'cause I come back eating.

Now, you get a heap of people talk about these stamps, these stamps, these stamps. "Oh, I could do without 'em." But let me tell you something about the stamps. They don't know what they're talking 'bout. If it wasn't for them stamps, one-half of us would be over yonder in the skull orchard. Be dead somewhere. Them stamps a help to us. They's a help to us. Now, hear some guy talking about, "I don't need no stamps." Yeah, you do. Now, don't let 'em get 'em, now, let 'em cut 'em off. If you would come back through here I would tell you who done pegged out. They need them stamps. Them stamps worth something. To me and all of 'em.

I want to tell you. The roughest time that I feel in my lifetime—and that's when I'm hurting and studying, wondering why I'm in this condition and when it is I'm going ever get well at the same time. I be studying when it is I'm going to get well and wondering why that I'm hurting this-a-way.

Now, these two boys live here. They ain't mine, they given to me. Now it's one, one of the boys, that bigger one, that's my sister's girl's boy, she give us him in '47. Well, in a way of speaking,

he was given to us 'fore he entered the world. I just tell you the truth.

Wife: She give him to me two month 'fore he was born. And then after he was born, that Thursday, and I come over from picking cotton, she called me and told me, "Annie," say, "here your boy." She was young and wild. Want to go. Didn't have time to fool with no children. And this other one, here, this little one, I'll tell you how we got him. He was four months old and he was sick. And my niece, she was wild, loose in the world, and didn't want to fool with the child. And when she brought me the child, child wasn't much bigger than that little stool over there.

Robert: I hope this—for my littlest kid—I hopes he will be a good, normal kid. And then I hope he'll get through with school. And, as he growing up, be careful with everybody, that's both black and white. I wants him to have a learn-

184

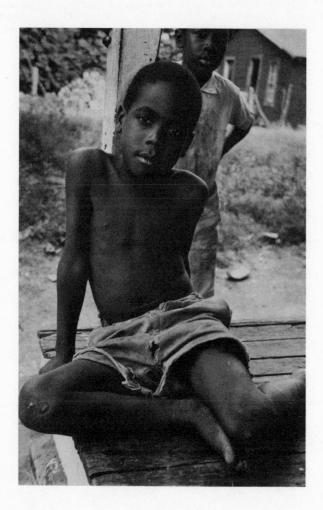

ing. Wisht I could get some aid for him, but it ain't no way do. No welfare. Just, Lord let me do the best I can for him. Let me live to see him get some kind of learning. You got to have that now. Yessir. Now you see, I'm just letting him go to school in vain. 'Cause the clothes he got. He just about barefooted now. And naked. I'm not able to give him clothes and shoes. Now, look, y'all can believe that. I'm talking what I know.

After he finishes school, I'll tell you what I wish he could get to do, get to be. I wish he could get to be a mechanic. 'Cause I likes that myself. I likes mechanics. That's what I hope for him.

Got in a little trouble a few months ago.

Well, just as usual, I'm a good old neighbor. I'll take anybody in my house. If I got a piece of bread, I'll give it to him. But now a lot of times—you heard talk of fattening frogs for snakes? Sometime you can fatten frogs for snakes.

This guy Kenny, he took this guy's pistol and carried it and pawned it. Stole it from him. And I kept the guy he stole it from from hurting him. But this Kenny, he was a bad guy, I didn't know it. I take him here one day. He broke in my chifforobe and takes sixty cents.

I've got a kind of soft heart, in a way. Sometimes I don't have no good heart. When they bother me. I went up there and told the sheriff. First, I said, "I tell you what I want you to do. Now I was good to that boy. I want you to keep him away from my house." I said, "I'm going kill him." And he said, "What you want me to do, Robert, arrest him?" I said, "No, sir, he ain't done nothing, let him alone. No, but just tell him to stay away from my house."

Then one cold morning, I was sitting up in that room right there drinking some coffee. Had my shoes off. And he come up here. And he was right out there and so my wife said, "Robert, that Kenny out there." I yells, "I don't want nothing of that Kenny out there. Ain't treat me right." And I said, "I saved his life. And saved him out of the penitentiary." Well, he told me, called, "Come here." And we went out there. And when we went out there he told me, said, "Gimme something to eat." Usually I'd give a person anything I got. But I told him, "I ain't got nothing." He started to walk off on me, he cussing and said he going kill me. Said he better not catch me uptown.

Well, ever since I arrived about fourteen years, I usually carried me a gun when I get up and put my clothes on. And I had to go get some salt up there in town. When he tell me that, he scared me, but I go up there anyhow. I had a solid fifty cents and than I had a

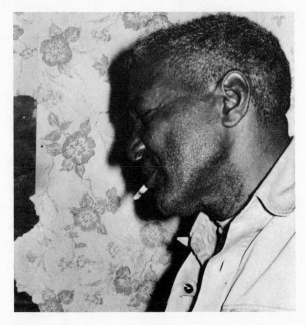

quarter. I went up there and I walked across that corner and there was Kenny and he grabbed me. I had on this coat. And my gun—see, he grabbed my sleeve, first this left-hand sleeve. He said, "Didn't I tell you I was going kill you and whip you?" I said, "You better not fool with me, else I'm going shoot you if you hit me." He was a kind of big old fellow. I don't care if he was that little, don't you catch on to me. I'll get scared, you see. He had hold of me. And wouldn't turn me a-loose. And I went to shooting him. That the way it went.

I got put in jail for it. Well, in a way of speaking, I don't care where you at, you know, quite natural the law going take its course anyhow. You got to be carried up, in a way, especially by law. I was taken in about seven weeks. But happen they turned me loose. Guy had a pretty bad rough name by his mama and everybody else. See, I didn't know the guy. That guy was kind of bad, they say. Turned me loose when they found out.

Well, if a person said he's going hurt somebody, ain't you going try to live? I'm scared of it. I'll be sick every day, hurting and that, but I don't want to die, y'all. Don't let a human in the world tell you I wants to die.

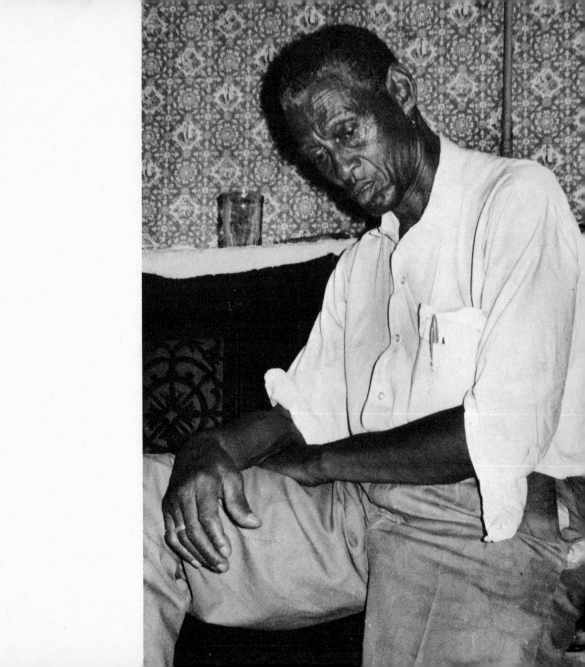

11/ *Go'n Sing This Verse,*
Ain't Go'n Sing No More

It was a dream, just a dream I had on my mind.
Well, I woke up this morning, not a thing could I find.

Well, I dreamed I was in heaven sitting down on a throne,
I dreamed I had a pretty angel laying back in my arms,
But it was a dream, just a dream I had on my mind.
Yes, I woke up this morning, not a chair could I find.

I dreamed I was in the White House, I was sitting in Mr. Johnson's chair.
I dreamed he shake my right hand, said, "Dewey I'm glad you're here,"
But it was a dream, just a dream I had on my mind.
Yes, I woke up this morning, not a chair could I find.

Well, I dreamed I was married, had a mammy for my wife.
I dreamed I was Rockefeller on my knees shooting dice,
But it was a dream, just a dream I had on my mind.
Well, I woke up this morning, not a penny could I find.

I rolled and I tumbled and I cried the whole night long,
Yes, I rolled and I tumbled and I cried the whole night long.
Oh, by morning I didn't know right from wrong.

What you want with a rooster when he won't crow 'fore day?
What you want with a rooster when he won't crow 'fore day?
What you want with a woman that won't do nothing you say?

Don't a woman act funny when she fixing to put you down?
Yes, don't a woman act funny when she fixing to put you down?
Says she gets to the place that she don't want you around.

I'm go'n snatch me a railing from your back fence,
I'm go'n whip that woman, try to learn her some sense.

          I'd rather see my coffin rolling
             up to my door.
          I'd rather see my coffin rolling
             up to my door
          Than to see my fair-brown say she
             don't need me no more.

    I feel like snapping a pistol in your face.
    Let some lonesome graveyard be your resting place.
    Well, I'm troubled, I'm troubled, all night long.
    You know I been worrying, worrying, baby,
        ever since you been gone.

191

Go'n buy me a bulldog to watch me while I sleep.
Got so many women, Lord, one may poison me.

Woman got a way, Lord, like a cat squirrel in the tree,
Everytime I lay, pardner, she jumping and dodging me.

Times I think, boy, my girl too cute to die,
Then again I feel like she ought to be buried alive.

Best woman quit you, don't you weep and moan,
Get another high yellow, boy, and you can carry that same thing on.

Going, I'm going, your crying won't make me stay.
More you cry, baby, further you drive me away.

Run here, baby, Lord, and sit down on my knee.
If your husband catch you, girl, I'll swear you kin to me.

'Way last night, Lord, when everything was still
Oh, me and my rider, Lord, we was doing the Master's will.

Ain't no doctor, I'll be the doctor's son.
Honey, I'll ease your pain, girl, until a doctor come.

Sometimes I sit and wonder
  How everything can change.
Well, I don't bother nobody
  that slanderize my name.
Jesus told me long time ago
Wheresoever I go
I won't have to make this journey
  all alone.
King Jesus is my captain
And He never have left me alone.
I am married to King Jesus
And we never have been apart.
I've got a telephone in my bosom,
I can ring Him up from my heart.
I can call Him on the air
Down on my knees in prayer.
Well, I don't have to make this
  journey all alone.

Lord, I want to die easy when I die.

194

Well, there's one kind favor I ask of you.
Yes, there's one kind favor I ask of you,
Just see that my grave is kept clean.

Lord, my heart stop beating and my hands got cold.
Lord, my heart stop beating and my hands got cold.
It won't be long till I'm in the shady grove.

Dig my grave with a silver spade.
Yes, dig my grave with a silver spade.
Just let old Johnny down with a golden chain.

Hearse come a-walking slow.
Yes, the hearse come a-walking slow.
You know old Johnny is no more.

Have you ever heard a coffin sound?
Yes, have you ever heard a coffin sound?
You know the poor boy's in the ground.

When I'm dead, don't grieve after me.
Yes, when I'm dead, don't grieve after me.
I just want my justice and my liberty.

I want to be ready when Jesus come.
Don't let Him catch you with your work undone.
I want to be ready when Jesus come.

Don't let Him catch you on the barroom floor,
Don't let Him catch you like He did before.
I want to be ready when Jesus come.

Don't let Him catch you in the gambling den,
Said He was coming but didn't say when.
I want to be ready when Jesus come.

Don't let Him catch you at the whiskey store,
Said He was coming, you will never know.
I want to be ready when Jesus come.

Sitting here wondering will
a matchbox hold my clothes?

196

My mother died and left me, it's been a long time ago.
Ever since my mother been gone, I been drifting from door to door.
Oh, now go down on my knees, talk to Jesus till I'm pleased.
Oh, oh, help me Father, stand by me.

My mother taught me from the Bible, sent me to Sunday school.
Now she gone and left me, don't want to break my mother's rules.
Oh, now go down on my knees, talk to Jesus till I'm pleased.
Oh, oh, help me Father, stand by me.

It was late one Friday evening, sun was almost down,
I did not have nobody on my burying ground.
Oh, now go down on my knees, talk to Jesus till I'm pleased.
Oh, oh, help me Father, stand by me.

When you see me coming, please don't close your door,
I'm a motherless child, don't have nowhere to go.
Oh, now go down on my knees, talk to Jesus till I'm pleased.
Oh, oh, help me Father, stand by me.

I'll kiss your soul
  and drink your blood like wine.

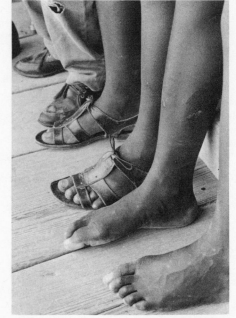

I'm a traveling man, mama,
  sure got a traveling mind.
I'm go'n buy a ticket,
  go'n ease on down the line.

Well, you don't know, you don't know,
  you don't know my fetched mind.
Baby, you don't know, you don't know my mind.
When you see me laughing, I'm laughing to keep from crying.

Well, I hit my woman, blackened her eye,
Would've cut her throat, but I scared she'd die.
You don't know, you don't know my mind.
When you see me laughing, I'm laughing to keep from crying.

198

You may take a boll weevil and bury him in the sand.
Say, in a few more days we'll help you break your land.

Well, I seen boll weevil sitting in a rocking chair,
Well, the next time I seen him he had a pencil behind his ear.

Well, boll weevil wrote a letter to the farmers in the South,
Said, "I will pick all of your cotton, won't come to your house."

Everybody begin to think boll weevil is gone,
He done pick all of my cotton, started cutting down my corn.

Well, I went to my merchant, asked for a little meat and meal.
Say, "No, no, partner, boll weevil's in your field."

Say, I went back, I went to get a little meat and lard.
Said, "I done told you, boll weevil's got you barred."

Crying ain't going down that big road by myself.
Now don't you hear me talking to you, pretty mama,
    Lord, ain't going down that big road by myself.
I don't carry you now, mama, gonna carry somebody else.

Sitting here a thousand miles from nowhere
  in this one-room country shack.
Yes, Lord, sitting here a thousand miles from nowhere
  in this one-room country shack.
But you know I have in my possession just
  an old eleven-foot cotton sack.

Well, I wake up 'long about midnight, people,
  just can't sleep no more.
Yes, I wake up 'long about midnight,
  I just can't sleep no more.
Well, you know I can't hear nothing but the frogs
  and crickets and the wind howling round my door.

Well, if I don't go crazy, people, it's bound to
  drive me out of my mind.
Yes, if I don't go crazy, people, it's bound to
  drive me out of my mind.
You know I got to have me some kind of companion,
  no matter if he's deaf, dumb, cripple, and blind.

200

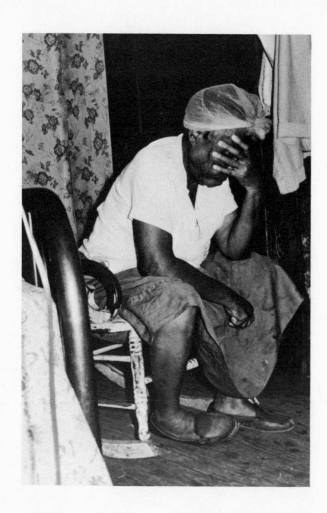

I've got the blues so bad
    it hurt my tongue to talk.
I've got the blues so bad
    it hurt my feet to walk.

I say black is evil,
It's always been my crave.
I believe to my soul black is going
    to carry me to my grave.

Never miss your water
    till your well run dry,
Never miss your fairer
    till he says goodbye.

Mama in the kitchen
cooking pork and beans,
Daddy on the ocean
running submarines.

Get a key to the Kingdom and then
the world can't do you no harm.
Yes, get a key to the Kingdom and then
the world can't do you no harm.

Now when you get in trouble, then
you know you haven't done no wrong,
Just call up central in Heaven,
can Jesus come to the bond?

Well, I asked for water and
she gave me gasoline.

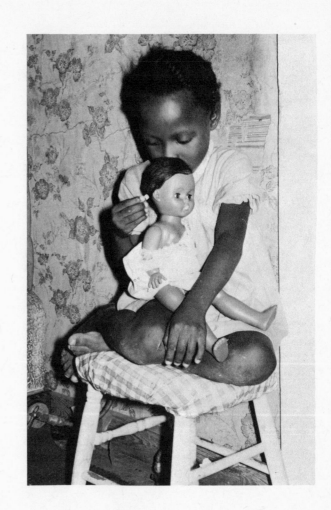

Motherless children sees a hard time when mother is gone.
Well, they'll do the best they can, but they just don't understand.
Motherless children sees a hard time when mother is gone.

Father won't treat you like mother will when mother is gone.
Well, he'll do the best he know, then you go from door to door.
Motherless children sees a hard time when mother is gone.

    Oh, the sun don't shine
      like it used to shine.
    It used to shine in your door,
      now it shine in mine.

Ever since my dear old mother been dead,
Rocks was my pillow, cold ground been my bed.
Yeah, rocks was my pillow, cold ground been my bed.

You know the nightmares jumped on me, oh Lord,
    they rolled me all night long.
Yes, the nightmares jumped on me, oh Lord,
    they rolled me all night long.
Yeah, I woke up and find nothing but a dream,
    that's why I'm singing this lonesome song.

I went home last night, sit down on my bed and cried.
Yes, I went home last night, sit down on my bed and cried.
You know I was thinking about my little woman,
    at the time you know I couldn't be satisfied.

I don't care where you go, little woman,
    I don't care how long you stay.
No, I don't care where you go, little woman,
    I don't care how long you stay.
Yea, them good old kind treatments,
    they'll bring a woman back home someday.

Did you ever wake up and your mind three different ways?
Yes, did you ever wake up and your mind three different ways?
Had a mind to leave and a mind to stay.

Well, I's born here in Mississippi
  and I'm easy to rule.
Say I was born here in Mississippi
  and I'm sure easy to rule.
You can hitch me to your middle buster,
  you can plow me like a mule.

Say I was standing on the corner
  just as drunk as I could be.
I was standing there on the corner,
  I was drunk as I could be.
Say Uncle Sam came driving along,
  he dropped his draft on me.

Well, I asked the conductor
  could I ride the blind.
Yes, I asked the conductor
  could I ride the blind.
He said, "Son, buy your ticket,
  buy your ticket, 'cause
  the train ain't none of mine."

205

Well, I done lost all of my health now, boy;
*   oh, I'm sinking down.*
Yes, I done lost all of my health now, Lord;
*   oh, I'm sinking down.*
Well, I don't want to give up no time of here,
*   oh, to live under the ground.*

I ain't going back to that Red Cross Store no more.
No, I ain't going down to that Red Cross store no more.

Well, those Red Cross people sure do treat you mean,
Lord, them cans of tripe, them old pork and beans.
That's why I ain't go'n let my baby go back to that Red Cross
*   store no more.*

Lord, I went to the merchant for some meat and lard.
He said, "Go away, boy, you know the times is done got hard."
That's why I ain't going back to that Red Cross store no more.

Lord, I went to the merchant for some meat and meal,
"Go away, boy, you know you ain't paid your bill."
That's why I ain't going back to that Red Cross store no more.

Time done been, won't be no more.

Sun go'n shine in my backdoor someday,
And the wind go'n blow my blues away.